Cont

Anyone with an interest in horses, in ranching life or in the Drewsey, Oregon, area will like this book. It is chock full of practical tips and tricks for keeping a rider and his horse out of dangerous situations, and for making life easier for himself and his horse. Furthermore, it contains good advice for would-be cowboys.

But the book is more than just advice and "how to do it" tips. It relates colorful experiences of an 83-year-old horseman. It contains tidbits of history I haven't seen written down anywhere: the beginnings of Frank Riley Horse Camp, the Skyline Trail Riders and many others. It gives a look into the day-to-day life of the ranchers in the Drewsey area. It is the culmination of Don Carlton's horseback days from 1919 to the present.

I met Don in 1975 when he rode up on his horse, Rusty Mia, to welcome my husband and me to the neighborhood. We had just moved into the small (at that time) community of Wilsonville, where many people had horses in their back pastures.

As I got to know Don, I found we shared an interest not only in horses, but also in Oregon's east side. Don was looking forward to retirement from his job as sales manager at Mayflower Farms in Portland, so he could spend more time horseback in his beloved country around Drewsey, Oregon. Don told me stories of cow punching for Drewsey ranchers and introduced me to their lives.

From 1948 until 1955 I had spent parts of each summer at my uncle Ellis Painter's ranch on Oregon's High Desert. He had a ranch near Sink, a long-deserted town between Fort Rock and Brothers. I had met Reub Long who co-authored the book *Oregon Desert* and knew many of the ranch folk in Reub's book.

As I heard Don's stories, I kept thinking they should be captured. He told how he had bridged the chasm between city life and ranch life, the ranch life that I knew on my uncle's ranch, the life that Reub Long talked about in his book. His tales of years on horseback trail riding in the mountains and deserts of Oregon showed me a wealth of knowledge that should be shared.

Don agreed to dictate his stories onto tapes. I transcribed the tapes and edited his stories for structure, but not for style. Don has a wonderful story-telling style.

Don's eye for detail brings his experiences to life. He takes us along on the trail rides around Mount Hood and around Mount Bachelor. We "see" a D-8 caterpillar hauling a Conestoga wagon up Mount Bachelor. We can feel the spine-shivering coyote song at Bluebucket Cow Camp as if we were right there. Don makes his experiences live.

Patricia Painter Kelley

This book is about horses, especially horses that go camping, go into the mountains, go into the desert or trail cattle. This book tells about making good and bad horses.

I have had saddle horses most of my life. I've ridden most of Oregon's Cascade Mountains and much of its desert. I have camped hundreds of nights with my horses and have trailed thousands of head of cattle.

From the time I picked up the reins on my first pony, Jumbo, when I was four, until today, when I am over eighty, I have seen good riders do strange things with horses, wrong things. I have seen intelligent, knowledgeable people unconsciously teach a horse bad habits.

Everything you do with a horse, right or wrong, is training. Say you get off your horse and stand in a group talking. The horse walks up to you to rub his head on you and steps on your feet. When that happens, it simply means that you've been a bad horse trainer. You are treating your horse as a pet.

I have a friend, Wil Howe, who is a horse trainer. Wil illustrates very clearly in his lectures on horse training why you can't make a horse into a pet.

Wil usually has a big stout colt standing beside him that is somebody's pride and joy and pet. He says, "Would you take your horse, whether it's a colt or an old horse that's well broke and well trained, and tie one of your hands to the saddle horn and let somebody else tie the other hand to a fence post, even if the horse was tied?"

Nobody in their right mind would do that. You are never quite sure what the horse is going to do. If somebody should happen to drop out of the sky in a parachute and land ten feet away, one of your arms or you and the fence post would be trailing down the road behind the horse.

Training a horse is a lot like teaching a child to brush his teeth or to wipe his feet. Every child has some basic habits and manners. Every horse should have some basic habits and manners. A well mannered horse is ten times the worth of a poorly mannered horse.

This book is about horses, but it's also more than horses. It's about campfires and good friends, too.

* * * * *

I was born in 1915 and grew up in Hoquiam, Washington. My dad owned and operated a dairy plant in Hoquiam, a town of about eight thousand people in those days. He made home deliveries of milk and butter and cheese by horse-drawn wagons. We had a barn, a big shed for the wagons and a pasture.

As soon as I was able to hang onto a bridle I got my first pony, Jumbo. I was four. Dad grew up on a ranch in Texas and he understood horses pretty well. He helped me. At age eight I graduated to Nellie, a gentle mare of about nine hundred pounds. I was born liking horses. I think most people who like horses are born that way. They do not acquire that feeling.

Hoquiam is on the Olympic Peninsula in Washington State, right on the coast. Around Hoquiam the hills start at the ocean's edge and push back and up until they become the Olympic Mountains. Hoquiam is at the south end of the Peninsula. Straight north is the rest of the Peninsula with beautiful lakes, mountains, and streams. We had a lot of rain. But in between the raindrops, it was beautiful country. Back then it was almost untouched except from the locals. I saw my first fresh bear track when I was not more than ten years old.

The trails wound through the wild mountains and I covered my share every day on Jumbo, later on Nellie. Usually my cousin, Del, rode with me.

We mostly rode bareback. But one day someone gave me a man's stock saddle to use. I couldn't get it up on my mare. A fellow around the barn there said he would saddle my mare and threw the saddle up for me and cinched it. I climbed aboard and headed for our house about four blocks down the gravel street. I kicked Nellie into a gallop and before I was two blocks from the barn, I plowed up the gravel road with myself. I was knocked out cold. Two women came and carried me around into our house. I lost some skin but I healed up.

That was my first lesson. The fellow who saddled Nellie drew the latigo up tight, but did not tie a saddle knot in it. The latigo worked loose and the saddle turned. I have not let anyone saddle my horse for me since. Too many people think their love for horses or a two-hour rental ride makes for experience.

When I was nineteen, mom, dad, and I left Hoquiam and went to Murfreesboro, Tennessee. The town was close to Shelbyville, which is the Walking Horse capital of the world. I got acquainted with Walking Horses and a Tennessee girl, Grace Ryan. Grace and I tied the knot.

After being in Tennessee for ten years, we were homesick for the Northwest. Dad sold out his share of the Red Rose Dairies in Murfreesboro and in 1944 we all came back to the West Coast.

I started working for Mayflower Farms at the Vancouver, Washington, branch. A couple years later I was promoted to branch manager in The Dalles. At that time, I bought a horse and spent the rest of my leisure time learning about, caring for, and riding these animals. That's what this book is about.

We moved to The Dalles in 1947. The Dalles sits right on the Columbia River just east of the Cascade Mountains of Oregon in hilly, desert country. Wheat and cattle ranches sit on the plateaus surrounding the town. The wind usually blows, down the river from the east or up the river from the west, but the area gets little rain, maybe thirteen inches a year. The sun shines most of the time.

I was in The Dalles about two months when I stopped at Red Harper's barn. Red traveled around with a string of horses—from The Dalles, to Toppenish, Washington, down through Morro, Biggs and other little towns in Oregon, buying, selling and trading horses. He also had a stable at The Dalles.

Pat, my five-year-old son, was with me. I got to talking to Red and missed Pat. We went to look for him. Chief, a big sorrel stallion, was standing in a box stall with a chain across the door. Pat had walked under the chain and into the stall with Chief. Chief had his ears laid back and was threatening Pat.

Pat stood in the center of the stall saying, "Here, get over there," scolding Chief.

Chief moved over. I about fainted. Red talked to Chief and to Pat in a slow easy way until he got into the stall, got his arms around Pat, and got him out.

Red had Chief altered and I bought him. After he was gelded, Chief was full of spunk but easy to get along with.

There's an old saying that when a stallion is altered (castrated), it's like brain surgery because it changes his mind. He changes from a hard-to-get-along-with animal into a nice, pleasant gelding. A stallion generally is unsafe to be around without knowing what you're doing.

Later on, I needed a horse for Pat and for my daughter Dianne. I told Red I wanted a good safe horse because I didn't want to be patching up the kids. I trusted Red completely.

Red said, "Don, I know an honest ranch horse, but he has a ringbone on his left front foot."

This was new to me, so he explained.

"Normally, ringbone is caused from an injury to the pastern joint (ankle) on the front foot. The injury causes the bone to extend and to grow. It grows around the pastern about an inch up from the hairline. You can feel the growth just above the hoof. It stiffens the pastern so the pastern loses half or more of its flexibility.

"If he's shod right, he'll be all right. And I can shoe him," Red said. "The owners are looking for a good home like you'd give him because he's been a good horse."

We went out to the ranch, close to Dufur, Oregon, in Red's old Ford truck and picked up Baldy. He was sorrel with a bald face and weighed about a thousand pounds. He was seventeen.

The way Baldy was shod when we picked him up, and the way Red shod him, was with the shoe on his left front foot shaped like a rocker on a rocking chair. Instead of hitting the ground flat, the heel hit first and rocked that foot on over. Shod with that rocker shoe, Baldy did not limp a bit.

Baldy taught Pat and Dianne how to ride. One day Pat and I came back from a ride. We curried the horses and were going to take them about a thousand yards to the pasture on the other side of the road. Friends from Portland had arrived who had a son about Pat's age. Pat wanted Guy to ride behind him to the pasture. The boys started out riding Baldy bareback on a dirt path alongside the road. Pat kicked Baldy into a trot to show off. Guy had his arms around Pat. They started to tilt to the left, got to about three o'clock, then hit the ground. Baldy stopped, looked back, cocked up his hind foot and waited for them to get up. This old horse was worth his weight in gold to us.

One winter with four or five inches of snow on the ground, Pat and I stopped by Red's barn. The wind was blowing. In the barn stood a brown and white pony that Red had traded for. He stood about thirteen hands and had a nice head. Pat liked him and began begging Red to ride the pony.

Red said, "Well, Pat, I'm not sure about him. I think he's a little feisty. Let's wait and you can ride him in a few days."

Pat could not keep his hands off the pony. He worked with him, picked up his feet, petted him.

He said, "Red, I think he's gentle. I think I can ride him."

He kept after Red.

Finally Red said, "Whatever your dad says."

Pat put his saddle on the pony and bridled him. We held the pony while he got on. The pony was working real well and Pat took him out into the pasture. I was talking to Red. Pretty soon I heard, "Whoa, whoa!" It was Pat. He and that pony were coming back to the barn going full speed. When they got to the barn, the pony put the brakes on and slid all four feet in the snow. Pat went over his ears, lit on his face in the snow and skidded about ten feet.

Red told him, "Listen, that wasn't the pony's fault. That was your fault. You never run a horse toward the barn. If you want to gallop a little, go the other way. If a horse gets in the habit of running toward the barn, and he'll get in the habit after you run him toward the barn about twice, he's going to be awful hard to talk out of running back all the time."

Many parents whose kids grew up in The Dalles between 1945 and 1960 didn't realize what a jewel Red was. Kids spent their days down at Red Harper's stables. Not a one went home without a horseback ride and learning something about a horse. By the same token, none of them ever went home without doing some work for Red. They cleaned the barn, shoveled manure or did whatever needed to be done. Red fussed at them and made them get their work done, but he always rewarded them with a ride.

Red didn't have much patience with people who didn't understand him, and it didn't matter that they might be customers. If he didn't like you, you had better duck. I learned many things from Red Harper who never attended much formal school, but had been to rough school all his life—the school of hard knocks.

One day I had ridden into Red's barn and was unsaddling. A fellow came along in a truck with a horse tied in the back. He stopped and exchanged greetings with Red and wanted to know if Red had a good saddle horse for sale. Red's eyes lit up and he trotted out his thirty or so horses. All the time the other guy left the horse tied in the truck. I thought to myself that Red should be looking the horse over if he was going to take him on trade.

They finally worked out a trade and the fellow unloaded the horse. Red never did put a saddle on the horse. The fellow loaded up his new horse and drove away.

Red looked at me and grinned. He said, "You know, that so-and-so thinks he really gypped me. But I've owned this horse twice before. He's cinchy as can be. Here, I'll show you. Let's see how bad he is."

Red picked up the saddle, threw a pad on the horse and set the saddle on. The horse stiffened up and his eyes got wide. Red tightened the cinch and the horse fell to the ground. He lay on his side, his legs stiff. His eyes rolled around, and he grunted and groaned. I'd never seen anything like it.

Red hollered at a little kid to bring him a Coke bottle full of water.

Red tilted the horse's nose up and started pouring water into one nostril. That horse scrambled to his feet just real quick. Red pulled the cinch tight again, and the horse hit the ground again, eyes rolling, grunting and groaning. Red poured a little more water in his nose. This happened a few more times and the horse got to where he would stand for cinching.

Red said, "Well, I broke him of it again."

Those early years in The Dalles I didn't have transportation for the horses, but I'd buy the gas and Red Harper would take his old Ford V-8 truck.

One hunting season Red, two other friends—Jack Ashby and Jim Howard—and I decided to go deer hunting.

Red, who knew the owners of the Corncob Ranch near Spray, Oregon, said, "I know those folks well and we'll go up there."

We threw everything together in a hurry. We borrowed a big army tent about sixteen feet square and threw it in the back of Red's truck, grabbed four or five bales of hay, the four horses, a big tank for water and whatever else we needed.

We took off with Red and me in the truck and Jack and Jim following in a car. I drove Red's truck. The truck was an old timer— a 1934 Ford one-and-a-half-ton truck. In the back were the four horses, hay, feed, all of our equipment and this great big army tent.

We got to the ranch and started climbing a hill above it. The truck had four gears and I had it geared down to first gear. We were grinding up the hill, just barely making it.

With the vibration, the gear shift jiggled loose and started floating around. The brakes were mechanical brakes and weren't too good. If the engine had stalled out, we'd probably still be going backwards down that hill. Someone had His hand on our shoulders.

We made it up the hill to about four miles behind the ranch. It was high open country, mostly sagebrush and junipers with a few pines. We found a fairly level spot and made camp. It was September and the year had been extremely dry. Fires weren't allowed except in certain areas and we were inside that area.

We started to put up our tent but discovered we hadn't brought the center pole. The center pole for a sixteen-foot-square army tent has to be about twelve feet tall. So we looked around. There weren't too many trees. Juniper trees, of course, are never tall and slender. There was no way we could use any part of a juniper tree. There were some big pine trees. We finally found a small pine. Being in dry country, it wasn't too tall, but was about six inches through.

We'd thrown one ax in the truck. It was so dull it took us forty-five minutes to cut that tree down. By the time we got it up, it seemed to weigh a ton. Lo and behold, it was too tall.

Jack said "Well, I'll be darned if I'm going to dig any more on this hard ground or try to cut that tree. Let's just set it up."

We set up our tent and pulled it out. The tall pole made the tent about ten feet wide instead of sixteen feet wide.The sides lacked about ten inches from coming to the ground. That tent sticking up there looked like a tall skinny man with real short pants on. You could see clear through to the other side if you bent over. When we were lying in bed we could see outside. It did protect us from the weather.

It was so dry that we couldn't walk without making a lot of noise in the leaves and duff on the ground. The next day we took the horses and covered a lot of country. About two miles above camp was some rimrock. It was steep but we got up there and could see where deer had bedded down. We decided to go back and spend the night. That way we'd be there before daylight and would stand a good chance of seeing some game.

That evening we ate our dinner and fed and watered the horses. We tied our sleeping bags on behind and rode the horses up to the rimrock. It got dark about six and we couldn't build a fire, so it was chilly. At that altitude we were cold. By the time seven o'clock came, there was nothing to do, so we crawled into our sleeping bags.

I went sound asleep. When I woke up, it took me a minute to realize where I was. I thought, by George, it must be about time to get up. I grabbed my flashlight and looked at my watch. I couldn't believe it. I looked again and my watch said ten minutes to eight. It was ten minutes to eight, still that evening. I'd been asleep about forty minutes. That was the longest night I ever put in. And cold. The sleeping bag I had was not good, a nine-dollar special from some place.

When we did hunt the next morning, we were lucky. We never found any deer, so we didn't have a deer to clean and fool with and take home.

2   *Small town camaraderie*

I loved the size of The Dalles and its location. I could leave my office and be home in five minutes, change clothes and be out at the stables riding my horse by five or six in the evening. Many times in the morning before I went to work, I'd go for a ride. There were trails everywhere and many horses in town.

On the west side of the Cascade Mountains a man cannot walk through the woods unless there's a trail. Around The Dalles we had large pine groves or juniper, but very little underbrush. I loved to ride in that wide open country.

We had a big saddle club—The Fort Dalles Riders. I made my first horseback mountain trip with the saddle club. We went up on the slopes of Mount Hood at Kneeble Springs, which was wild, beautiful country with many trails.

I belonged to Kiwanis International. Two other members were weekend cowboys like myself. One was Harold Sexton, the sheriff, whom I rode with quite a bit. He had a big white horse named Rex that he rode in parades.

Among the Kiwanis Club, someone was always playing a joke on someone else.

Del Martin owned and operated The Dalles laundry. Del had a sense of humor you could see a mile away. I'm sure his eyes twinkled at night. He and Charlie Roth, the fire chief, had a good-humored feud going. One would pull something on the other and it would go back and forth, back and forth.

Charlie had the number one fire department in the State of Oregon. He was dedicated to his job.

I was branch manager of Mayflower Dairy where we bottled milk. Our plant was on First Street. Del's laundry was a couple of buildings to the east. Right next to Mayflower on the west was an old building that Del owned, which had been closed. It was dilapidated and Charlie had been on Del to tear it down.

But there was one problem. There were two old Chinese men who dated back to the early times in The Dalles. One of them was Lee; the other one was Hop-Sing. Hop-Sing and Lee lived in the old building. It was a good-sized building and inside they had built a little hut they lived in.

It was a fire trap and a thorn in Charlie's side.

Del would say, "Charlie, I can't tear it down. What am I going to do with old Hop-Sing and Lee?"

Charlie would say, "I don't know, but you've got to do something."

This had been going on since before I came to The Dalles. One day a fire got started in their little hut in that building. The fire department came and put it out, but it left it in shambles inside. Here were these two elderly Chinese men, who were part of the history of The Dalles, out of a home.

The day after the fire, I got to work about seven in the morning. Dumped on the street in front of Hop-Sing and Lee's old building was a whole truckload of building stuff—lumber, a keg of nails, shingles.

I thought to myself, "Good Lord, is Del going to rebuild that building?" Then I didn't think any more of it.

Pretty soon the phone rang. It was Del.

Del said, "Don, do something for me."

I said, "Sure, whatever I can."

He said, "Do you see that pile of lumber out there?"

I said, "Yeah, are you going to fix that place up?"

He said, "No, but I want Charlie to think so." He was chuckling. He said, "I want you to call Charlie and complain bitterly about that pile of lumber out there. Tell him you won't stand for Del fixing that place up. Charlie's going to come down here and we'll have some fun with him." He said, "You better come on over about two seconds after you hang up that receiver because it's going to be hard for you to beat Charlie down here."

So I called Charlie. I said, "Charlie! What in the world are you thinking of?"

He said, "What do you mean?"

I said, "Del's got a big pile of lumber right up there in front of Lee and Hop-Sing's place. He's evidently going to rebuild it."

He said, "You're kidding."

I said, "No, I'm not kidding. It's a big pile."

He hung up and I hung up and I ran over to the laundry and

ran downstairs below the office where I could listen to the whole conversation.

No sooner had I got down there when Charlie skidded up to Del's front door, jumped out of his pickup and ran in. He said, "Del, what in the hell are you up to?"

Del said, "What do you mean?" He sounded innocent as a lamb.

Charlie said, "That pile of lumber. You can't fix that place up."

Del said, "I can't turn old Hop-Sing and Lee out. They've got to have a place to live. I'll fix the roof and they can kind of fix that place up in there."

Charlie had a fit.

Del said, "You know, Charlie, I've just got to fix it up. You can understand that, can't you?"

Charlie said, "Yeah, I can, Del."

Del said, "Charlie, we've been friends an awful long time."

Charlie said, "Del, I'm going to do my duty."

Del was just busting his buttons trying to keep a straight face.

Charlie said, "Besides that, you can't get a building permit because Homer Wall isn't going to give you a building permit on this." (Homer was the city engineer.)

Del said, "Oh, I've already got my building permit."

Homer had entered in on the joke and had given him a building permit.

Charlie almost went through the roof.

This thing went on until about the same time the next day. By this time the whole town was in on it.

Here, Del Martin and Scurv Scurving, the manager of Tum-a-lum Lumber Company in The Dalles, had gone to the expense of hauling this over just to have that fun. It was not just a few sticks. It was a whole truckload of lumber, nails, shingles and everything that went with it.

One of my customers owned Johnny's Cafe in The Dalles, Johnny Wannaluck. Johnny and John Steele, who had an insurance business in The Dalles, were good friends and great fishermen and sportsmen.

It's hard to catch a trout in the Deschutes. There are a lot of them in there, but you have to know how to get them. Johnny and

John would always have a display of trout in the window of Johnny's Cafe. They'd catch some real beauties: rainbow trout, nice ones, three or four pounders. They also hunted.

On the last day of deer season they went hunting.

They went up behind The Dalles and parked at the end of a road on a kind of knob there. John went one way on one point and Johnny walked out the other way.

Each of them shot a doe, but only Johnny had a tag. They weren't sure what they were going to do. They'd noticed a car parked back on a little fork of the road so they went back there.

A guy was in the back seat asleep. They knocked on the door and he barely stirred. They looked in and saw a half full fifth of whiskey lying beside him. He'd drunk himself to sleep. They knew the fellow.

There happened to be a doe tag in this guy's pocket. They took the tag and tied it to one of the does, put the doe in the front seat, propped it up at the steering wheel, tied the front feet to the steering wheel and left it. The guy slept right through it.

That is life in a small town. There is so much fun.

The time finally came. My boss at Mayflower Farms took me to lunch one day. I knew he had something on his mind and I was afraid of what it was.

Gene said, "How about coming into the main office?"

I heaved a sigh. I was being asked to leave and go to Portland.

Gene said, "I know you like it here. We never tell anyone that they're going to be transferred. This is up to you; it's your decision."

It was a better job and a real chance for my career. I knew in my heart that I was going to accept it. I just couldn't tell him that right then. I didn't want to go.

I said, "Gene, I've got to think this thing over."

So I spent a week not sleeping very well, talking to Grace, talking to my kids. Grace didn't like The Dalles as much as I did. She liked Portland better. After much soul searching and anguish, I transferred into Portland.

The day I left The Dalles I cried. I hated to leave. The five years I was there I enjoyed to my soul.

In 1952 we moved with our two horses, Chief and Baldy, into
Garden Home, a small community near Portland. We had a hard
time finding a place we could afford and still keep two horses. But
we found a house with a small barn and a large corral. We rented
an acre of pasture across the road.

From where we lived, I could ride across the road then down
a trail into the Portland Hunt Club. The Hunt Club let the
neighbors come in and ride their half-mile track. The old Oregon
Electric Railway right of way to the Coast ran by the Hunt Club.
The railroad tracks and ties were gone so it made a terrific
horseback trail. Just over the hill further west was Nichol's Riding
Academy. Alex Williams was running the Academy.

One Saturday morning I was riding Chief, my big red sorrel
gelding, and Dianne was riding Baldy along the Oregon Electric
trail. We met a fellow riding a spotted mare so we stopped and got
to talking. It was Guy Beck on his mare, Ginger. He lived not
more than half a mile from us. Guy and his wife, Lessie, had come
from Alabama to Oregon a few years earlier. He was a mechanic
and the foreman in the Mack garage.

We were friends from the start. Ninety percent of Guy's
recreation was around horses and the outdoors. My kids loved
Guy, and Grace and Lessie hit it off.

One day Guy told me he and some friends were going to haul
the horses up to the old Barlow Trail on Mount Hood and camp for
a long weekend. He asked if I would like to go. I jumped at the
chance.

I didn't have a trailer, so I rented a single-horse trailer. We
went up to Gate Creek, on the east side of Mount Hood. Guy's son,
Bob Beck, and two other fellows came along: Chuck Davis and one
of his employees, Dorsey.

We got in early on a Friday and set up camp. We had a cook

stove but not a tent. We rode all that day on the Forest Service fire roads throughout the area. That night we had a big campfire. I was in hog heaven. Big dinner. Big stars. Good weather. Horses on the picket line.

Guy had cleaned out his horse trailer and said, "I'm going to sleep in my horse trailer in case it rains."

I had cleaned out my trailer just in case I had to sleep in it. But I told him, "It doesn't look like rain; I'm going to sleep under the stars."

I rolled out my new sleeping bag under a big pine tree and crawled into it. I was tired from the long ride and went to sleep immediately. I woke up during the night and it was sprinkling. I was under the tree, but a raindrop or two hit me in the face now and then. I reached back and pulled the flap of the sleeping bag up over my head, turned over and went sound asleep.

About four in the morning I woke up. It was raining pitchforks and I could feel myself getting wet. I had a brand new cowboy hat, and, boy, was I proud of it. I'd bought it for two bucks. When I went to bed, I laid it beside the bed and put the rest of my clothes under the sleeping bag. There was my nice green straw hat all wet. It was soft and limp.

It had been raining hard for quite some time. The ground was wet and muddy. Here I was in my underwear, in a sleeping bag that was getting wet and the rain still pouring down. I thought I'd stay and stick it out, but it got wetter and wetter.

The water started coming into the bag. I finally got up, got my clothes in one hand, put that wet soggy hat on, got the sleeping bag and air mattress under one arm and stumbled barefooted over to the horse trailer and threw my stuff in. I got into the trailer, got a towel and dried off. The next morning the sun came out. I spread my sleeping bag out and dried it. I slept in the trailer the next two nights.

This was my first good exposure to being out where we made our own camp. There were no tables, no fire rings, no anything. We were next to a stream. I loved it. I hated for the hour to come that we had to leave. In that trip I found what I wanted to do in my leisure life: ride horses and camp with them.

Guy's close friend, Paul Ford, was an old Wyoming cowboy. No one knew him by Paul; we called him Whitey. He'd spent more time on a horse in his life than he ever had in an automobile or pickup and had the bearing of a cowboy. He had cowboyed in

Wyoming, Nevada and Oregon. At one time he worked for the great old ZX ranch, the largest ranch in Southern Oregon.

Whitey was a true-enough cowboy and a good one, although somewhat heavy handed and hard on a horse's mouth. But a horse didn't come too tough for Whitey. He would ride anything that came down the road.

Whitey had a melodius voice. As we rode along, he would sing old cowboy songs one verse after another. I don't think I ever heard two verses the same. He must have made them up as we went along. They were songs I hadn't heard before and haven't heard since.

Whitey had given up cowboying and gone to work for Pacific Power and Light Company as a high-wire man. He climbed light poles and did the work up at the top. But his heart was still in cowboying. He lived not too far from Guy and me and had a little

Don Carlton and Whitey Ford at Frank Riley Horse Camp, 1964.

Art Middleton, U.S. Forester and his pack string, in the Idaho wilderness about 1925.

ground where he kept a couple of horses. He always kept a good horse and had one up until the day he had to have one of his legs taken off due to diabetes.

I remember very clearly Whitey's big, good looking buckskin gelding named Keno. Keno was quick and fast and, in the right situation, would throw you over a tree.

Guy, Whitey and I rode together a lot, especially on that old Oregon Electric trail.

Whitey's wife, Ethel, came along on many of the camping trips.

Stan Maves, an insurance adjuster for Safeco Insurance Company rode with us. He and his wife, Joyce, lived on acreage outside of Beaverton. He kept a half-Arab half-Quarter horse mare named Kim. At times he had other horses as well. At that time the mare was running in about fifty wooded acres. Kim was one of the toughest horses I've ever been around. She could go on any trail and go forever. Stan had Kim until she was almost thirty years old. Stan's pole barn, which he built himself, was a second home for us.

Art Middleton, a retired State Forester from Idaho, was one of the best outdoorsmen I have ever known. He was born around Hagerman, Idaho, and went to work for the Forest Service when he was seventeen years old. He furnished his saddle horse and a pack horse and got sixty dollars a month for himself and the two horses. That was pretty good money in those days, about the late 1920s.

Art taught me a lot about the outdoors. One time we were camped in the Metolius, which is beautiful open country on the east side of the Cascade Mountains. It has sparse pine trees, lodgepole pine thickets, juniper trees and sagebrush.

We had camped at Sheep Springs and had ridden quite a ways from camp. I usually took a compass, but this time I didn't have it with me. The clouds came in and wiped out the mountains that I used for directions. I got confused; the country all looked the same.

I said to Art, "I hope you know the way back to camp."

He said, "Well, Don, you just want to remember one thing. Look at these great big pine trees around here, especially those that are not in a cluster, maybe three or four that are kind of by themselves."

I looked at the trees, which were about one hundred to one hundred fifty feet tall.

He said, "Look at the long branches on those trees, do you see anything?"

I said, "No, not really."

He said, "All the long branches point to the south. They are growing toward the sun. This is a natural phenomenon."

So I learned that if I ever lose my bearings, especially in Eastern Oregon where there are big pine trees, I can pick out three or four and most of their longest boughs will be pointing to the south.

One weekend Art, Stan and I hauled our horses to Frank Riley Horse Camp on Mount Hood. We got away about noon on Friday and got into Horse Camp around one thirty.

There was one outfit in there. They were out riding, but it looked like they had four horses with them. They were camped across from where we normally camped. No one was in the spots where we usually camped, but they were roped off. Someone had written "reserved" on a piece of cardboard and taped it to a piece of the rope.

I looked at Art. Art said, "It looks to me like we were here first."

I said, "I agree."

We took the ropes down, coiled them up neatly and hung them on the branch of a tree. We backed our rigs in and unloaded our horses. We put up our picket lines and set up our camp. After we got everything set up, Art said, "Here, you guys, I'll pour you a drink."

Art gave us each a bourbon and water, one to Stan, one to me and one for himself. We each held a pretty good-sized drink full of ice cubes. We were standing there and four guys rode in horseback.

Art Middleton stood six feet four inches tall and weighed two hundred twenty pounds. He wasn't fat but he was big. He had hands like hams. Art must have been sixty at the time.

One of the riders, who looked about thirty years old, tied up his horse and came charging over. He started to eat us out from one end to the other for taking down his reserved sign. He said, "We had this place all reserved. You gotta get out of here."

Art started to say something, but the guy wouldn't let him. He just kept on talking and getting madder.

Art threw his drink right square in that fellow's face as hard as he could throw it. The drink hit the guy's face so hard that one ice cube hit him on the forehead and bounced ten feet in the air. It surprised him. His mouth was open and he was spouting bourbon and water.

Art said in a very quiet voice, "Son, don't talk to me in that tone of voice."

The guy looked at Art, looked UP at Art, spitting and sputtering; he didn't know what to say. He turned around and stomped back over to talk to the other three guys. They took a look at us but nothing was said. I don't think we spoke to them the rest of the weekend.

On that same trip, we had a big picnic table loaded with food. We'd been partying a little bit. Art came galloping through camp and jumped his horse clear over that table with all the food on it. Art was not careless; he just felt so good to get back out in the woods. He knew more about the outdoors than the rest of us put together and he knew horses.

Denny Wells and his wife, Eula, lived in the northwest part of Beaverton. Denny loved horses and riding like the rest of us. He rode a King-bred black Quarter horse by the name of King, an excellent animal.

About this same time Johnny Adair started riding with us. Johnny and Pearl lived up on Germantown Road in Northwest Portland.

On the Paul Lewis ranch: Tony Lewis mounted on the horse, Don Carlton, Paul Lewis, John Adair, Guy Beck.

Guy Beck and I were with Johnny on the Paul Lewis ranch on the Deschutes River when Johnny bought Rocky, a big Quarter horse colt. Rocky was a tremendously tough, good horse, but he'd buck every once in awhile. I saw Johnny take some rough rides on Rocky, but he was a terrific rider and he understood horses. Johnny rode Rocky until the horse fell and broke his leg when he was about twenty-two years old.

Sid and Donna Murray came just a little later in the last part of this era. At the time I met Sid he was riding Sky, a nice looking black Quarter horse, although more Thoroughbred than Quarter horse. Sid and Donna lived in Gladstone.

In the 1950s and 1960s this was our basic riding group.

Art and Myrtha Middleton, Grace and Don Carlton, Stan and Joyce Maves at Todd Lake Meadow, 1967.

Not long after we moved to Garden Home, the kids wanted a horse livelier than Baldy. We sold him to a couple who wanted him for their small children.

I bought Bonnie, a good looking strawberry roan mare. She was powerfully built, with a wide chest and big hindquarters. She stood fifteen hands tall and weighed eleven hundred and fifty pounds.

Bonnie was a bit balky. When she didn't want to go some places, it was pretty hard to get her to go. She turned out to be somewhat spoiled and I wasn't that experienced a horseman at that time. I was thinking about selling her.

It was my son Pat's chore to feed the two horses each morning. One morning he went out to feed and came running back. I was eating breakfast, getting ready to go to work. I'll never forget the look on his face when he came in. He was about nine or ten at the time. His eyes were as big as dollars. He said, "Daddy, daddy, there's a new colt out in the corral. Bonnie is the mother and I found it and it's mine."

He whirled around and ran out the door. Of course, we all piled out to the barn and corral. Sure enough, here was a little gray colt, brand new, standing and nursing Bonnie.

We didn't know that Bonnie was in foal because she was so stockily built. I just thought she was a little bit fat. The people who sold her to us didn't know she was in foal either.

Pat was virtually beside himself. He went through that fence before I could stop him. Bonnie laid back her ears a little bit. He ran up to the colt and she let him get right in there. I opened the gate to go in. Bonnie flattened her ears back. Here was Pat in there petting the colt and she didn't care about that, but she didn't want me or anybody else around that colt.

Pat, again, claimed the colt, so the colt was Pat's.

We raised the colt until it was a little over a year old. We could tell it was going to be smaller than what we wanted. We found some people who fell in love with the colt. It was Pat's colt and Pat got the money for it.

That was the first colt we owned and it was a good experience. Since that time, I've decided that it's easier to look around and buy a good four- or five-year-old horse that hasn't been spoiled.

We found another mare for the kids. Shy-Anne was a good looking sorrel with a white strip, a couple of white feet and well built. The kids rode her for a long time. She was a nice quiet mare, but she was a mare.

I've heard so many people buying a horse for the first time say, "I had a mare when I was a kid," or, "We had horses and I want a mare; I know about them," or, "I want a mare so I can have my own colt to break."

An inexperienced person breaking their own colt is like me flying a 747 from here to Tokyo. It is ridiculous. They raise the colt like a pet and spoil it to death.

Also, raising a colt is a long process. It takes about a year by the time you buy the mare, get her bred and get the colt on the ground. Then you have to wait until the colt is strong enough to ride. Although some people start colts at eighteen months, that is too young to be riding them. You can put a saddle on them, work with them on the ground and get them used to everything. But a horse should be two or two and a half years old before he's mounted.

A big guy who weighs one hundred ninety to two hundred fifteen pounds should not be getting on a young horse. The horse's bones aren't set and could be damaged trying to hold up a big man. Even a big colt's bones are soft. Perhaps a young person or someone of around a hundred pounds won't cause problems. But you get anyone any heavier on a young horse and you're going to have problems.

If someone absolutely has to have a colt or young horse, the best way to get one is to take in one of the sales and look for the weanling colts. You can buy a good registered Quarter horse colt much cheaper than it costs to breed and raise one. And you know what you're getting.

You can write for a catalog ahead of time and study everything that's going to be for sale. You can go see the colts, get an idea of how big they're going to be, what kind of feet they have and so on. You'll know who the sire is, who the dam is and how big they are.

The colt is probably seven or eight months old and ready to wean. He's usually halter broke but not spoiled. You can take him home and work with him on the ground.

I think the best using horses are those who have passed the seven year mark. They have some of the foolishness and giddiness out of their system and are a pleasure to ride.

Although I have owned several mares, over the years I've grown to believe that geldings make the best pleasure saddle horses. A gelding doesn't worry about anything other than himself, eating and doing what he has to do.

Perhaps one mare out of one hundred is different. You wouldn't know she was a mare unless you looked. But most of them can be real problems on the trail or in camp.

A mare comes in season—in heat—every month. During that time she often is a little on the cranky side and apt to kick. I've had friends with mares who have been kicked numbers of times when their mares were in heat. Maybe they had forgotten to say something when they walked up behind and startled them.

I do think a mare is a little smarter than a gelding. They learn quickly. Some good horsemen feel that a mare makes an excellent ride because she is smarter and learns a little faster.

I have a story on mares. A bunch of us were up in the mountains camped with our horses, riding for pleasure. We went to bed one night and, oh, boy, a mare started squealing and whistling. She kept it up all night. You could hear her pawing. I was thinking it was my friend's mare and she usually wasn't that bad. The next morning we got up and looked out. There stood a mare we all recognized, but that wasn't with our group.

Her owner was camped about five hundred or more yards away. He came over to get the mare. The mare had dug a hole about a foot and a half deep. Her front end was that deep in the ground where she had pawed all night long and squealed and whinnied.

My friend said, "Hey, so and so, what are you doing with that horse over here? She kept us awake all night."

He said, "Yeah, I know. She does that every night. I just had to get a night's sleep. I thought if I tied her with your horses, she wouldn't be so noisy."

This fellow was a real nuisance. He would somehow or another always find out where we were going on a week's trip or a long weekend and he would show up.

On a trip into Todd Lake Meadow for a week's vacation, we set up our camps and picket lines. We were camped on the edge of the meadow and could see across the meadow to the dirt road that came into camp. I looked across and here came our friend. I knew his pickup and his horse trailer. He pulled in and made camp. He was riding an overweight paint mare, which was not well trained.

The next morning when we all set out for a ride, our friend showed up on his mare with clothespins on her ears.

I said, "Hey, what in the world are you doing with clothespins on your horse's ears?"

He answered, "This mare doesn't like to walk. She jigs and dances. I read in a magazine that if you put clothespins on a horse's ears that it would take the horse's mind off the jigging so it would walk."

I said, "Does it work?"

He said, "No."

We went on up the trail into upper Todd Lake Meadow. Here were some people I knew—the man I had sold a horse by the name of Carlos to. We stopped at his camp. He kept eyeing Paul's horse with her ears out sideways and clothespins dangling from them. Finally he couldn't hold his curiosity any longer. He said, "Mister, how come you got clothespins on that horse's ears?"

Paul told him what he had told me.

Sam said, "Does it work?"

He said, "No."

Everybody just busted up laughing.

Stallions can be worse than mares. I don't think it's a good idea to try to make a pleasure horse out of a stallion. If the old timers like Reub Long or Herman Oliver were here they might argue that. They often rode stallions in their day. In fact, around the turn of the century, it was macho to ride a stallion. But both Reub and Herman knew there was a big difference between a working ranch horse and a pleasure horse.

In their day, the pastures were thousands of acres. The horses were worked, sometimes daily, and probably every other day. That makes a lot of difference in a horse. Those of us who earn our living in some way other than ranching or horseback spend forty to sixty hours a week on our job and ride horses on the weekends. Sometimes we don't get to it every weekend.

Very few pleasure horses get exercised enough through the

week. They are usually standing, some of them in box stalls, being turned out a few hours a day or a few minutes a day. If we had a stallion penned up that long between rides, we would have trouble. And you can't turn one loose in a pasture unless it has a tough, high fence around it.

I've never liked to go camping with someone who had a stallion. If a mare in camp was in heat, the stallion was whinnying and whistling all night. He might jump the fence or do most anything to get to the mare. It's hard to take a stallion and go into a strange horse camp, especially if you are all alone, as I sometimes am. I unload my horse and tie him to a picket line.

I don't think it's a good idea to try to make a pleasure horse out of a stallion. The chief purpose of stallions, in my opinion, is to raise little horses. You see lots of stallions at horse shows simply because the owners want an outstanding stallion to be seen by other people. For breeding purposes, they have to first prove their worth in the show ring or in cutting, or, especially, on the race track.

I've heard some people say, "Oh, I ride a stallion. You'd never know it; you'd think he was a gelding."

It doesn't stay that way. I had a friend who always rode a Quarter horse stallion. The horse was quiet and nice and you would think he was a gelding if you didn't know it. Even around a mare in heat, he wouldn't cause any trouble.

One day we were camped up at Logan Valley on a sheriff's posse summer ride. There were probably two hundred people and one hundred fifty horses.

The man with the stallion took his feed tub, put grain in it and took it out to feed to his horse. He set the feed tub down in front of him. When he did, the stallion reached around and grabbed the man by the neck and jerked him off his feet. He tore the skin loose from the front of his neck and you could see the jugular vein. His teeth just missed everything in there.

By this time the fellow was on the ground. They rushed him to the hospital and got him fixed up. That was the very first time that stallion had ever misbehaved.

It's interesting to me that the US Cavalry, as near as I can tell, never had a mare or stallion out on the line. They had to have a horse they could picket at any time. They had mares and stallions in their remount stations to raise horses to get more propagating stock, and to provide stallions to geld for good riding horses.

Most ranches today keep their big strong mares and never do more than halter break them. They run them in the hills with their stallions and raise their colts this way. For doing their daily work, they keep a cavvy of geldings to ride. There are exceptions, no doubt about it, but for the most part this is true.

A gelding can be ready almost any time and he hasn't got his mind on anything else other than grass and the next time he's going to be ridden. If I were buying a saddle horse today, I would not be interested in a mare, period. I would look for a good gelding.

This bears itself out. Good geldings are in such demand that it takes someone who really knows what they're doing to go to a public sale and buy a good gelding. Not many people want to sell good geldings. They keep their good ones and sell the sour ones or the ones that don't do so well or the ones that are unsound.

If you go to a big sale, say the Hermiston sale in Oregon, or one of the Outwest Sales—Ted Billingsley and Chuck Simmelink— you will find good geldings hard to come by and they bring a bucket of money.

It's easy to go to a sale and pick up a gelding that is either unsound or spoiled or has very bad habits. Probably the best thing to do is to buy a good two or three year old that somebody hasn't fooled with and take him to a good trainer.

In 1960 the kids were getting into high school. My son Pat and I decided to build a boat and I decided to quit horses. We sold our house on acreage and moved into a subdivision on the edge of Beaverton.

Pat and I built our boat in the garage. It took about six months. We had a kit for a fifteen-and-a-half-foot boat with a deck. We did a good job on it, fiberglassed the whole thing. I put every gadget it could have on that boat. We skied on it and took it fishing, although the motor was a little too big to fish with.

Art Middleton kept two horses to ride so he'd have one to ride if one got sick or lame. Art's favorite horse was Bill, a big good looking Quarter horse with a strip in his face. He was a King-bred horse. He weighed probably twelve hundred and fifty pounds and stood fifteen hands high. He also had a horse named Toy Joe Bailey.

He told me, "Don, you'd do me a favor if you'd come over and ride Toy."

Toy Joe Bailey was anything but a Toy. He was a registered Quarter horse of Joe Bailey breeding. He was well built and well broken. We would go camping and Art would bring Toy along for me. I didn't miss a ride.

I was riding his horse so much that I decided to get my own saddle. I went up to The Dalles to the Kuck and Bonney Saddle Company. Garth Bonney, the sole proprietor, was an old time saddle maker. I had him build me a saddle. I broke in that saddle on Toy.

Pat and Dianne Carlton on two good geldings, Ribbon and Big Tommy Tucker, 1953

Problem horses

In 1964, I was captain of the Multnomah County Sheriff's Posse. The sheriff's posse was basically a drill team. Half the horses were black and half were palomino. We all had black gear, real sharp looking outfits. It was during this time that I bought Carlos, a seven-eighths Thoroughbred and a palomino. He was just six years old, a good looking son of a gun and a fast walker.

Carlos made a good drill horse. He had had some good training and was quick and responsive. He was a bit high strung and a snorty horse. There were times I wasn't sure if maybe he was too much horse for me. But we always got along well. I was quiet around him. A guy could have stirred him up to where he could have gotten into real trouble. When I got Carlos I was about fifty years old and old enough that I had to be careful of what I was getting on because I hit the ground pretty hard.

I had known Carlos for a long time. The Posse worked out at Greentree Stables and the people at Greentree Stables owned Carlos. They were showing him English and jumping him. He got to be a pretty good jumping horse and they showed him a lot. He was doing real well. They called him Mr. In Between.

But when I bought him, I answered an ad in the paper and it was a horse shoer. I went over to Portland Hunt Club to see the horse. When he brought the horse out, I said, "Say, I know that horse. Isn't that Mr. In Between?"

He said, "Yeah, that's the horse they owned over to Greentree. I bought him and I've been going to do some jumping on him, but I haven't had time to ride."

So I got on him. When I rode off, Carlos was walking so lightly it felt like he wouldn't have broken a dozen eggs if he had been walking on them. He had a little hump in his back. I knew that if I made a sudden movement, he would start bucking. I also felt that if I took it easy and warmed him up a little, he would be all right. And that's the way it worked. The tenseness came out of him and the saddle came down an inch or two in the back.

He was a quick horse with a good rein on him. I would just touch him with a rein and he would spin around. I had to sit tight on him and turn with him or he would have left me out there in the green pasture.

After I bought Carlos, I took him back over to Greentree Stables. When I put the saddle on him and got on, he had that little hump in his back and I had a short rein on him. I was not about to let him get his head down.

The ladies who owned Greentree and one of their daughters happened to come out to the ring. I saw the mother nudge the daughter and point to Carlos. I could tell they were in a real discussion. As I rode him around, they watched me closely. They expected me to get unloaded any minute, to take a high dive on Carlos.

I rode him around the ring a few times. They stood there talking. I stopped and said, "Well, folks, do you recognize him?"

They said, "Sure."

Carlos wasn't mean. Somewhere along the line, he had been mistreated. I think Carlos had been handled in a rough way. Some horses will take that; some won't. Carlos was definitely the kind of a horse that rough treatment would drive up the wall.

I have never been rough with horses. I make them mind. I am firm, but I am quiet. When I'm around horses, I'm always talking to them, always trying to do something a little extra so they are used to anything in the world. I got every horse I owned to where I could put a yellow slicker on in a windstorm with it flapping around his head. A horse gets used to anything if he trusts you.

Carlos trusted me. Of course, not right away. At the first drill I rode him through, it was all at a canter. Guy Beck, who was riding in the same drill, said, "Don, Carlos was just half bucking all through the drill."

Carlos had been in a box stall at the Hunt Club, so I didn't have an inkling of how hard he would be to catch. At the time I was boarding the horse with my good friend, Guy Beck. He had five horses in his barn. Guy let them all out into a big pasture.

When I went over to catch Carlos, I threw a little grain in the tub to coax him into the stall. But it didn't work. I opened every stall door in the barn and opened the big door in front. I put a little grain in every stall. Then I kept the other four horses in their stalls. Here would be Carlos peeking around the corner of the barn. Here I would be in the barn in the feed room peeking around the corner waiting for Carlos.

That son of a gun would run in, try to get a mouthful of grain and run out before I could close the door. Half the time he would get it done. He about drove me crazy trying to catch him. I had Carlos for over a year and never spent less than half an hour trying to catch that hummer.

If I could just get my hand on top of his neck, right on his poll between the ears, he would stand still and let me put the halter on him. That's the way he was trained. But he was also trained that when a guy went out to rope him, he was always looking the other way.

After being around horses for many years, I felt that I could always break a horse from his bad habits. I found out that some horses are impossible. Such was Carlos. I got so tired of trying to catch that horse, that I sold him. I hated to because he was one of the best horses I ever had.

I sold him to a friend who was a polo player. He used Carlos for playing polo for many years. Years later we were all camped up in the mountains and his daughter was riding Carlos. At that time Carlos was about eighteen years old and he was still kind of hard to catch.

Frank Riley was the one who had brought Carlos to Western Oregon. Frank had bought the horse from Carlos Parton, a rancher in Eastern Oregon. Frank had a habit of naming his horses after the person he purchased them from. He sold Carlos to Greentree Stables, so Frank knew his background and told me his name was Carlos.

Carlos Parton is in a picture on page 232 in Herman Oliver's book, *Gold and Cattle Country*. It shows a scene of heading and heeling branding of calves taken about 1920 on Herman's ranch.

I met Herman Oliver several times, the first time at a Chamber of Commerce meeting where he was the chief speaker. He was a great old western rancher and excellent speaker. I have read his book probably ten times.

"That horse is a walker. Man! He walks," Frank said. "I'll tell you, Don, where he came from he had to walk fast because it was a long ways between spears of grass."

Carlos had been a ranch horse. They would keep a wrangle

Carlos and Don Carlton preparing to ride in the Portland Rose Parade, June 1964.

horse in and let the rest out. Then a man would go out in the pasture, round up the horses on horseback, and run them into the corral where they would rope them. This had trained Carlos to be hard to catch.

Because Carlos was running loose with other horses, I could not break him to where I could catch him. If I had had him at home in a pasture by himself, I am sure I could have broken him of that bad habit.

If you train a horse to run away from you when you're trying to catch him, by gosh, he's not hard to train.

When I go to catch my horse at my place, I don't just grab a halter and run him down outside. I first go into the barn and throw a handful of grain in his feed tub. It doesn't have to be much, just a tiny sprinkle. A horse doesn't have the kind of mind that says, "Well, I'm only going to get just a touch of grain so I won't go in there."

My horse comes in and goes right to the grain. He doesn't reach over and pick at me for the grain, which he would do if I were feeding him out of my hand. He stands and waits at his feed tub if he beats me in. If I want to keep him in, I go over and put the chain up across the stall doorway while he's eating.

I always feed my horse in his feed tub so he always comes to the barn. If he likes carrots and I want to give him a carrot treat, I take it down and put it in his feed tub. He stands in front of his feed tub and waits for the treat rather than nibbling on me or chewing at my shirt sleeves or jacket trying to tell me, "Hey, you forgot my treat."

If you feed a horse by hand, you are training him to do the wrong things. Every time you come up to him, he expects a handful of oats or an apple. If he doesn't get it, he's disappointed. He'll reach over and grab at you, nip your shoulders. If he does that long enough, he's going to get you in his teeth along with your clothes. You'll get a nice coat or shirt ripped because he's picking at you, looking for his treat. If you smack at him, that's all you'll ever do. You'll be swinging your arms at him and he will dodge.

If you are going to reward a horse, throw the treat in his feed tub. If you have just shucked twelve ears of corn, take them down and throw them in his feed tub. Do not feed them to a horse by hand.

I believe to my soul that if you go down to the barn every day, especially on days when you're working around the barn cleaning things up and not trying to catch the horse, and throw a handful of grain or a few carrots or some treat for him in his feed tub, that the horse will get to where he comes in.

I know this would have worked for Carlos. At first he would have peeked around the corner for an hour before he came in. He would have sneaked up, grabbed some grain and run back out again. With nobody chasing him trying to catch him, he would have slacked off on that. Pretty soon he would have come in, gotten his treat and relaxed while he was getting it.

I would gradually have gotten him used to me going out of the stall and coming in from the other side. He probably would have left and I would have walked on out under the overhang and fooled around out there a bit.

The first time that he came in and relaxed and I caught him, I would have curried him, cleaned out his feet, talked to him a little then turned him loose. It wouldn't have taken long for him to relax and come in and I would have had a horse I could catch. But as long as he was running with other horses, I couldn't teach him.

If I were on a ranch and had a large corral, I would have a feed trough in the corral. Instead of sending a wrangle horse out, I would set up a little grain feeding every morning. It would not have to be much.

Every horse on the place would come in when they saw me go down there with that feed bucket. I would put out some grain where they all would get a little and close the gate. I think that's a whole lot easier than saving a wrangle horse, saddling him and going out and rounding up the horses.

Except for Carlos, I have never had a horse I could not walk up to out in the pasture. You train a horse to be hard to catch if you go out in the pasture with a halter and run after him. He gets pretty wise when he sees you coming with a halter or bridle or rope. He'll go as far as he can. If you get him in a corner, he'll put his head in the corner and turn his rump to you.

Many people turn horses loose with a halter on because they have a hard time catching the horse. I would not turn a horse loose in a pasture for even ten minutes wearing his halter. Many horses have been crippled for life or died as a result of having a halter on.

They'll reach around with their head and use their hind foot to scratch it. If the foot gets caught, it hangs up in the halter. The hind foot does not have to have a shoe on it either. A bare hind foot can get caught in a halter just as quick as one that has a shoe. I have seen it happen twice and I have heard of it happening many more times.

If the halter doesn't break when a foot hangs up, the horse is going to go down. A halter would have to be pretty weak to break because the horse can't exert much pressure on it when he's caught in that position. If someone doesn't see him and free him, he's not going to live more than an hour or two after he goes down. If it happens at night, you will have a dead horse in the morning.

He can get the halter hung up on a fence as he reaches around the corner of the fence to get that juicy tidbit of grass that he sees there on the other side. If it hangs up in a firm place, the halter is going to break, or the horse is going to scratch himself up or he is going to end up wound up in the fence.

After Carlos, I bought Sandy, a good looking, big gelding who was quick and catty. I knew the man who sold him to me, Ben Weiler of Weiler Chevrolet Company in Oregon City.

Ben told me, "Don, this horse has been spoiled. The kids got to racing him back to the barn."

I said, "I can break him of that." I was sure I could.

Ben said, "He's a good horse, and I'll sell him to you. But if you want to get rid of him, just bring him back and I'll give you your money back."

I kept Sandy about a year and I never made any headway. One weekend we camped at Frank Riley Horse Camp. We spent one whole day up in the hills. It was steep, rough country and the horse should have been tired. But when I hit the flat and got about four or five miles from camp, Sandy was switching sideways, prancing, his knees up and down under his chin, wanting to run for home. He would have bucked if I'd let him.

Someone might look at him and say, "Oh, isn't he pretty. Look how proud he is with his neck and head up."

It might look good in a parade, but it's the bunk for a pleasure horse. I want a horse to do what I want it to do, not what the horse wants to do.

Sandy and I went back and forth on that several-mile stretch of path at least four times. We would get almost back to camp and I would turn him around and walk him back the four miles to the Muddy Fork of the Sandy River. Going away from camp, he was the perfect horse. I would have to poke him along with the spurs. I would turn him around towards camp and there he would go again, knees up, dancing sideways.

I had decided to take the horse back to Ben but some people who were camped there liked him because he was so stylish. I knew the people and knew they would give him a good home. I sold him while we were camped there. I was at the end of my expertise in getting Sandy out of that bad habit.

I learned over the years that if you are camped and are coming in at a gallop, you go at least half a mile by camp. Then turn the horse around and walk him back to camp. Even then you are taking a big chance on letting a horse acquire the bad habit of running toward home.

A few summers ago I spent four or five days up at Frank Riley Horse Camp. Two couples were camped across from us, very nice young people. We got acquainted with them. We moved some of our vehicles so they had room to camp.

Late in the afternoon I happened to be down the road a quarter of a mile on a sandy stretch across Lost Creek from the horse camp. A sandy fire road runs about three miles along Lost Creek. Around Mount Hood there are millions of rocks but the ground is sandy and loamy.

I heard some horses running as hard as they could run. I looked down the road and coming around the corner were those four young people, two men and two women, racing back toward camp. They were really flying.

They saw me and pulled up their horses. They had a hard time getting them stopped. One of the women went by for about one hundred fifty yards before she could get her horse stopped. She came back. The horse was extremely excited, jumping sideways, up and down.

We talked a minute. I tried to be diplomatic. I said, "Hey, you know, running your horses back toward camp like that sure spoils them quick."

One of the women piped up and said, "Oh, I know. But my horse just loves to run back towards camp."

I didn't say anything. What else could I say? The horse is probably spoiled for life. That is the hardest bad manner to break that I know of.

There is one thing about horse people. It seems almost anyone who ever puts in as much as four hours horseback is an expert.

Over the years I have learned a trick or two about teaching manners to a horse . Not many horses are born mean. A mean horse is usually a high-spirited animal that started training very late with a trainer who didn't know what he was doing. The result is a mean, vicious animal. Stallions are different, though. You do have to be careful with even the best trained stallion.

Too often people make pets of their horses, But they are too big to play with. If you try to play with a horse, he'll run up to you and maybe try to put his hooves on your shoulders. Many times I have seen a horse whose owners have played with him run up, then whirl, kick up in the air and run away. It's a dangerous game. Those heels could catch you in the face.

Sandy, a barn sour horse.

The average saddle horse likes attention. A horse that comes up to you and rubs his head on you is lonesome or bored. Many people feel the horse is their best friend when he backs up and scratches his shoulder or his head on their back. But rubbing is a bad habit and you should not let your horse do it. If you do, this thousand-pound horse is going to rub on you whenever you are standing close to him. If a fly lands on his head, instead of shaking it off, he is going to scratch it off on your back or shoulder.

We have all seen the cartoon of the cowboy standing looking straight at the horse and the horse standing on both of the cowboy's front feet looking him right in the eye. That's not what you want. The horse should be careful of your feet. You should not have to worry about keeping your feet out from under him, although you always watch it, of course.

The ideal horse never tightens the lead rope or reins by pulling back, and you never have to tell him to get back because his breath is in your face. When he is being led, he should stop when you stop.

Something that happened as I was dictating this book

illustrates my point. I have dictated all of this book into a recorder and I usually go out into my motorhome to do my recording. I was out in the motorhome working on this book when I heard a female voice saying, "Don, Don!"

I stepped out and saw it was my new neighbor from up the road, Hannah, a young woman about twenty-one or so years old. She was leading her newly purchased three-year-old registered filly. The filly was acting up.

Hannah said, "Don, help me."

I took the horse and led her down to the barn where I picked up my little leather bat with a leather popper on the end of it.

I took the halter rope and worked with her. When she acted up, I worked her chest over good with the bat. It didn't hurt the filly; she probably didn't even feel it, but the popper on the bat made a lot of noise.

I made her back up about fifty feet in my driveway. Then I said, "Come on." She started running ahead of me. I did the same thing with the bat again.

After five minutes with her, I made her understand that I was in control. I walked her back down the driveway and she followed me quietly. I handed Hannah the rope and said, "Hannah, you just have to be firm with her. You don't have to hurt her, just be firm."

As we talked for a few minutes, the filly reached over and was picking at Hannah's blouse with her mouth.

I said, "Hannah, don't let her do that."

She said, "That's all right."

I said, "What do you mean?"

She said, "My trainer told me that I shouldn't let her bite me, but it's all right if she just nuzzles my clothes because it means she loves me."

Hannah was teaching a new filly bad habits with this so-called trainer's advice. It would have been so easy to teach the filly good habits.

So how do you keep a horse from walking all over you or pulling you down the path when you are trying to lead him or trying to walk around him?

Ground work is the ticket. This means working with the animal on the ground. It's not hard. Even a horse that has been spoiled changes his mind if you work with him.

Don't just throw a saddle on him on the weekend and ride

him off. If you only throw him hay twice a day and then go out and work with him once a week, it's pretty hard for him to keep manners in his mind. Give him some consistent training.

Even a well-trained horse picks up bad habits. You might purchase a horse that has had excellent training and has very good manners. Unless you help him, he won't maintain those habits. It's important to work with him several times a week. He forgets what he has learned unless you keep putting him through his paces.

Every day or two put a halter on him. Take him out in the pasture and lead him around. Make him stop when you stop, go when you go. If he wants to prance out in front of you, stop and pull him down hard with the lead. Jerk on his nose and scold him.

Make him back up. Have a short whip, a quirt or a leather bat with a popper on the end of it, something about two-feet long that you can use to smack him on the chest or legs if he is getting too close. Smack him on the neck if he starts to rub his head on you. An upward pop on the bottom of the chin that he can't see coming gets his attention and does not make him head shy. Just work with him. You will be surprised what a little bit of work can do.

If you clean his feet three or four times a week, it teaches him that you are the master, you are the boss. Maybe his feet do not need cleaning that often, but it's good for him. When you bring him in and tie him up, he has to stand quietly and do whatever you want him to do. Most horses that are hard to shoe are simply horses that have not had their feet fooled with much.

A rancher asked me once, "Don, how is it that when you bring a horse up here you can rope off him without any trouble?"

The reason is that before I ever touched a rope when I was on him, I got him used to it from the ground. I tied him up to a tie rail and started twirling the rope. He ducked and shied from it. Pretty soon he didn't pay any attention. Then I threw it over him. He jumped a little bit.

Gradually, I threw the rope anywhere I wanted to on that horse. He knew it wasn't going to hurt him. I threw it around his back legs, threw it around his front legs, threw it around his head, caught his neck, did everything I could do with a rope. Pretty soon, he took a little nap while I was throwing the rope around. It is so easy to get a good horse used to things.

I used a gunny sack full of empty tin cans. The more noise it made the better. First I worked with him from the ground. Then I got on and dragged the sack of cans behind me. I pulled it up alongside the horse and down the other side. The horse got so used to it, he almost went to sleep.

If a horse didn't want to do something, I would do it until he liked it. You have to be in charge. If a horse wants to turn to his left, turn him to his right. If he wants to turn to the right, turn him to the left. Get him used to doing the things you want him to do.

A horse should never turn his rear to you and it's an easy habit to break. Use a three-quarter- or half-inch braided cotton rope. Any time he turns his rear to you, smack him as hard as you can across his rump. It's not going to hurt him. It makes a pop and gets his attention. He will turn around and face you. If he is in a stall and turns his back to you and puts his head in the corner away from you, stand where he can't lash out and kick you and smack him on the rump. He soon learns that the way to keep from getting smacked is to face you.

I cannot remember any established horse camps in the early 1960s in Oregon. It was through the efforts of OET and some dedicated people that we have many fine horse camps now.

Oregon Equestrian Trails, or OET as we called it, was a horsemen's group for people who liked to get out in the outdoors and ride. Saddle clubs throughout the state belonged to OET. OET worked with the legislature and the US Forest Service to get horse camps.

Earl Flick, the first president of OET, was so dedicated to seeing horse camps and horse trails built and maintained that he was elected year after year to head OET. He was president for twelve or fifteen years. All the horsemen in Oregon owe Earl a vote of thanks.

Frank Riley Horse Camp was the first horse camp in Oregon. It's on Lost Creek on the west side of Mount Hood. It's sixty miles from Portland—about an hour and a half drive when you're pulling a horse trailer or using a truck with a horse van and a travel trailer.

This horse camp was started by and named after Frank Riley. It was through Frank's pushing and begging and cajoling that we got the horse camp.

Frank, a retired cattle and hay rancher from Goldendale, Washington, stood about six foot two and weighed around two hundred pounds. He looked like a cowboy. If you put a tuxedo and all the trappings on Frank and put him in the middle of the floor with strangers, nine out of ten of those people would pick him out for a cowboy.

When I first met Frank, he was living in Gesham. He had bought property on Mount Hood and had put in a string of thirty or forty dude horses at Zigzag. He also had a string of ten or twelve big Missouri mules and packed for the US Forest Service in the

Mount Hood district. Frank kept his mules and saddle horses in the Forest Service horse barns. Everything that went into the wilderness area, everything that went up those trails for the Forest Service including the Forest Service crews went on Frank's pack string. Aside from doing all the packing at Mount Hood, Frank rented out the horses.

Frank had no fear of any horse and there was no horse he couldn't handle. He would get some mean ones, but he knew how to take advantage of their bad dispositions. Frank didn't let a horse get too far having his own way and he knew his stuff. Sometimes he was a little rough with a horse, but he had some rough ones to tame.

In the early 1960s he bought a big red sorrel horse from a guy who couldn't handle it. The fellow sold him to Frank for about two hundred dollars. He was a good looking Saddlebred, but the horse was mean. He'd been mistreated, I'm sure. He'd buck a rider off in a minute. Frank rode Red for one summer in the mountains. From then on Red was in the dude string and gentle as a lamb. Kids or anyone who didn't know horses could ride him.

Frank's favorite saddle horse was a big Thoroughbred named Hobo. That horse was at least sixteen hands and probably weighed thirteen hundred pounds. He was one of the best and one of the toughest trail horses I've ever known.

Frank was president of the State Association of Mounted Sheriff's Posses. He, Guy Beck, Sid Murray and I belonged to the Multnomah County Sheriff's Posse.

All the sheriff's posses in northwest Oregon got together and helped build the Frank Riley Horse Camp. Two or three fellows in the posse were contractors. They brought up heavy equipment— backhoes and so forth—and dug trenches to put in water lines. The Forest Service dug out a big spring up on the hill and brought the water down to Lost Creek. Then we brought it on over to the horse camp. It was just about the purest water in the world, nice and cold always.

Water is the one thing you simply have to have when camping with a horse. You can carry enough water for people, but you cannot, unless you have a tank truck, carry enough water for horses. They drink too much. All established horse camps have water in the camp or nearby.

The water piped into the camp was distributed to four different faucets. A huge hollowed-out log at the far end of the campground

Don Carlton, Frank Riley, Guy Beck and Dianne Carlton at the St. Helens Rodeo, 1963.

served as a watering trough. We had two or three outdoor toilets, but no showers or hot water. The camp had about twenty individual camp spots.

The posse members also poured a big concrete slab about twenty-five feet by thirty-five feet. This was the dance floor where we held our parties.

The Forest Service was insisting that we build a big place down at the end of the camp to keep all the horses. Frank dug in his heels.

He said, "Listen, I know these people. No horseman is going to take his horse into a strange place, take him five hundred yards away and tie him where he can't see him. We have to build tie racks at every camp. Otherwise these people will not bring a horse in here. They want to be close to their horses, especially at night when anything can happen. A bear or an elk or a deer or any wild animal could come into camp and spook the horses."

Frank went toe to toe with the Forest Service on this. They were really dug in and so was Frank. Frank won the argument and they built stalls at every camp.

Frank was one hundred percent right. I know few horsemen

Don Carlton on Carlos, Denny Wells on his mare and Stan Maves on Kim out for an early spring ride on Mount Hood, 1964.

who would go into a camp, put their horses out where they couldn't
see them on a picket line and leave them. As much as I love that
horse camp and like to go up there, I would not have gone the first
time if I had had to leave my horse.

In the beginning each camp had tie rails for two horses, one
to be tied on each side. Then they changed that to a cross of two
rails. This made four places to tie four horses. But tying horses
this close is not always good. When horses are tied, they get bored
and get to picking at each other. Pretty soon one bites another,
then the other whips around and tries to kick. A horse can get
damaged. Even horses that are kept together a lot get into trouble.

We spent many happy camps at Frank Riley Horse Camp.
Since 1972 I have kept a journal on all our trips that we've taken
in the trailer. As I go back through those journals, I can see that
Frank Riley Horse Camp is the horse camp we used most. And we
have been to all of the camps in Oregon many times.

Frank Riley Horse Camp is right up against the west side of
Mount Hood, the rainy side at the thirty-five-hundred- to four-
thousand-foot level. Mount Hood peak rises to 11,000 feet just east
of the camp.

When the clouds come in from the ocean, they push up against
Mount Hood, dump their rain, then either disintegrate or go on
east. If it is going to rain any place in the State of Oregon, it's
going to be at Frank Riley Horse Camp. No one ever rode out of
that camp without a slicker tied behind the saddle.

In spite of the wet, there are some good rides out of Frank
Riley Horse Camp. Horseshoe Ridge trail is probably the best ride
now. This trail travels about a mile southwest out of the camp
along Lost Creek. It fords the creek, which is not a problem. At its
deepest, Lost Creek is not over two or two and a half feet deep.
Horses in the Northwest are used to water. But they have to be
shod well because there is a lot of rock.

The trail then goes up the mountain along several
switchbacks, crossing a large shale slide on the side of the
mountain. It is very steep where it crosses the shale slide, about a
sixty degree angle. The trail goes across the slide, switches back
across the slide, switches back across the slide again and switches
back one more time at the top. After the third switchback we could
look out and almost straight down. We could see the whole country
down below, covered in huge fir trees.

I'm a person who has never been very brave when it comes to

heights. A horse's back is about as high as I like to get, or a short ladder. I always had to kind of mentally grab hold of myself in this place. It did bother me looking down.

On that shale we really watched what we were doing and kept a good hold on our horses. The trail is dug into the shale, but a lot of horses have a tendency to walk with their hind end out a little bit. I am sure anyone who has ridden in the mountains has experienced this: you're on a trail with a steep drop-off on one side and the ground gives way beneath the rear foot of your horse and the foot slips off the trail and down. Although the horse has three other legs and feet on the trail, it does give you a little thrill.

This is where a good trail horse makes a big difference. I never wanted one of those goofy horses that wants to dance half the day instead of walking, or one with his head stuck way up in the air. I want a horse that has his head down, one with a headful of sense. He is looking at where he is going, at what he is doing. He isn't crammed up against the horse in front of him, and he isn't laid way back where the horse in front is forty feet away either.

From the top of the shale, the trail goes down the other side of a ridge and into two little mountain lakes: Cast Lake and Dumbbell Lake. We usually ate lunch there.

Coming back down, we'd take Cast Creek trail, which was pretty much straight downhill and very very steep. There were some places where it would have been better if it had had some switchbacks. I never rode a horse up that trail. A two hundred pound guy and fifty pounds of saddle and gear on a horse and going up that straight is too tough and hard on a horse.

I never ceased to be amazed at the ease that a horse can come down a steep trail with a rider on his back, though. But then I stop and think about how a horse is made. His hind legs and hind feet are made to go up under him. So when he goes down a steep hill, his back is darn near level. It really isn't level, but he takes a lot of the steep out of it. If his back was at the same angle that the steepness of the hill was, it would be hard to keep from going over the horse's head regardless of the saddle.

One of the first times I came down Cast Creek trail, I was riding with Guy Beck. At one place Guy got off his horse and led him. He led the horse for about twenty feet. The horse was sliding all over Guy and he was having a hard time. He stopped and turned his horse sideways to the hill and said, "You know, this horse has four legs and I've only got two. I think he's handling this hill better than I am and I'm going to get back on."

Guy got back on the horse and that was the last time he ever got off a horse going down a hill.

Cast Creek trail comes out on a fire road, which is about a mile or so above Frank Riley Horse Camp. From there it is an easy ride back to camp.

In the early days, we could get into a place called Eden Park, which is about eleven miles from Frank Riley Horse Camp. It is above the timberline and in a beautiful canyon with springs everywhere. There are a couple of tough places in the trail to Eden Park. Cathedral Ridge is one of them.

Five of us were on our way into Eden Park one day. We crossed the Muddy Fork, crossed the other Muddy Fork and went on up toward Bald Mountain shelter.

About a mile on up from there was Cathedral Ridge. The trail wound up and went along the top of the ridge. We could look down into the gorge that dropped down eight hundred feet. It was steep and deep. At that point we were at about seven thousand feet in elevation, right at the timberline.

We could see across to the other side of the mountain above the timberline; it was a pretty sight, all snow and rocks. We could see the snow glaciers of Mount Hood.

The ridge trail wound through a thicket of noble fir. Because it was so high, all the trees were stunted.

I was in the lead riding my black gelding, Gentleman Jack. We were making good time, clicking right along. Here came a group of hikers the other way with backpacks on. The fellow in the lead had tied his shirt to the top of his pack frame, which was about at head level. There was a stiff wind blowing—there always is on the mountain there—blowing from behind him and towards us.

As he came around the corner, the first thing that came around was his red shirt, sticking straight out in that wind. Man! When Jack saw that shirt, things happened. Gentleman Jack was a big horse, but he was quick and catty. He swapped ends so fast that I didn't know what happened. I certainly did not go with him.

It seemed like I sat in the air for a minute or so then crashed on down. But I never hit the ground. Noble firs were growing thick and they all were stunted. I lit on those and the brush growing beneath them. It was just like landing on a featherbed. I never did have a jolt. It was hard to get out though because there were so many trees.

Another ride out of Frank Riley Horse Camp was a nice easy trail to Ramona Falls, about ten miles round trip. The posse cut out the trail and blazed it. The trail crossed a fork of the Sandy River, then wound around to a crossing of another fork of the Sandy. These crossings are both called the Muddy Fork. The Muddy Fork got its name because the river comes off the mountain so fast, drops so fast that, although it is pure snowmelt water, it carries a lot of sand in it.

The first crossing wasn't bad. It usually was clear so we could see the bottom. We could get into it and cross it square.

Almost all the rest of the water was as clear as the air up there, but the Sandy River at the second Muddy Fork crossing was sandy. You couldn't see the bottom so you couldn't tell how deep it was. There were places where the dirt had washed out from around the rocks so the footing was just big rocks, some of them jagged and sharp, some of them round. Your horse couldn't see where he put his foot.

On a stream that has a rocky bottom, especially one with big rocks, and those rocks ranged from the size of a baseball up to the size of a man, I always liked to see the bottom of the stream. We couldn't do that in this part of the Sandy River. This was another place where I wanted to be on a good trail horse.

A good trail horse feels his way through. One that's not used to the fast-running water gets scared and tries to lunge his way through the river. That's when you can get into trouble. If he steps in a bad place, he can go down with you. Besides getting wet and awful cold, it's dangerous because of those rocks. Of course, good trail horses aren't born; they are made by good riders. You take an inexperienced horse up there and put him with a couple of good quiet horses and a quiet rider who doesn't get excited, and he'll learn to handle a stream like that, to cross it carefully.

Once across the second Muddy Fork, a four-mile circle goes into Ramona Falls. At the falls, there is a small three-sided shelter and a place for a fire. It is a great place for backpackers, hikers and horsemen. This was always the lunch stop on that ride. You could drink the water at Ramona Falls. It was ice cold, good water.

Another ride out of Frank Riley Horse Camp went into Paradise Park. It lies above the snow line on the south side of Mount Hood and is accessible from camp by trail only. It's a beautiful ride into a natural park. Although it's above the snow line, it isn't barren. It has two or three snow streams running

Horse riders crossing the Muddy Fork of the Sandy River on Mount Hood, 1964.

through it with a few stunted trees.

As we rode into it, we had a beautiful view looking out toward Portland. We could also look down and see the Three Sisters and Mount Jefferson in the southern part of the Cascade Range.

There was one tough spot on that trail that I disliked—a stream called Roaring Creek, and, believe me, it was a roaring creek right out of the mountain. It was only about six feet across and four feet deep where we crossed, but we were on rocks. They were mostly big rocks probably weighing a ton, with some small ones, some jagged and some round.

Because of the rocks, it was too dangerous to try to jump. The landing was so uncertain—very uneven, different angles, and other treacherous places with those rocks.

By the same token, it was the same way in that water. I felt a horse could easily break his leg there. I never heard of one breaking a leg going across Roaring Creek, but it looked bad. I was always glad when I got across that and back over it without any problems.

After our rides, we had a cocktail hour in the evening. Many times people came into the horse camp who were good musicians and a party developed over at the dance floor. Bill and Eleanor Daffron were horsemen and musicians. Bill played the string instruments and Eleanor played the accordion. Or some of us brought tapes, backed our rigs up to the dance floor and turned up the volume. We would dance on that concrete floor in the moonlight. We had some good dances there.

The nights were cold almost any time of the year, so we usually had a big campfire going. So many wild stories were told around the campfire. Of course, the kids would always have marshmallows and wieners.

I enjoy sitting around a campfire. The fellowship and camaraderie that are part of a campfire are pretty doggone hard to beat.There's something about a campfire, too, that brings on low voices. It's almost like it's confidential.

There are many other fine horse camps in the State of Oregon other than Frank Riley Horse Camp due to the work of Earl Flick and other people, but mainly Earl and OET. Sheep Springs and Graham Corral horse camps are about one hundred forty miles from Portland in the same area east of the Cascade Range. Both are on the Windigo Trail, which goes from the Metolius River south up into the Three Sisters mountains and into the Skyline Trail.

I have left many times from Portland in a heavy rainstorm, and maybe snow going over the pass, even in late June. Then five miles down the other side, the clouds would start to thin out. Ten miles down the other side, the sun would be shining and the highway dry. That seems hard to believe for anyone who is not used to this country. But when you get to the east side of the mountains, it makes a terrific difference in the weather.

Sheep Springs is an old sheep camp on the Metolius River

Bill and Eleanor Daffron playing the dance music at Frank Riley Horse Camp.

behind Camp Sherman. We have been going there since before it was a horse camp. Art Middleton took me in there for the first time and I fell in love with it. It's beautiful, rather flat country. Because it's on the east side of the mountains, the timber, mostly pine and juniper, is not nearly as thick as that on the west. We could ride in any direction without obstacles.

The old sheep camp had a nice big spring where water came up out of the ground, which is common to this area. The water in this country, which is right in the heart of the Cascades, is coming out of the ground from the snow, which is going into the ground on the mountains.

The biggest spring is the one that makes the Metolius River. The mouth of the Metolius River is ten miles from Sheep Springs. It comes up out of the ground and from there on it's a river forty to sixty feet wide that flows down to where it empties into Billy Chinook reservoir. It flows that way year around. It's a wonder of nature, to me anyway, that that much water comes out of there. It's a fast river, ice cold, and good to drink up close to the springs.

Graham Corral is right on the Windigo Trail and only two

miles off the Santiam highway, just eleven miles west of Sisters. It's an old sheep camp, but with corrals for horses. It has good ice cold drinking water.

Three Creek Meadow is about seventeen miles due south out of Sisters, Oregon, on the north side of Tam McArthur Rim and North Sister Mountain. It is a nice horse camp at about sixty-two hundred feet in elevation. We had beautiful riding out of there into Park Meadow and Green Lakes and all the way to Sparks and Elk lakes. Good trails also led up over McArthur Rim and down into Todd Lake and Todd Lake Meadow.

Two herds of elk always hung around in there.

The only thing wrong with Three Creek Meadow is that when the wind came out of the north, it cut right through us. It made a campfire feel good. Most of the time the weather was good. We just took warm clothes.

Quinn Meadows is probably one of the nicest horse camps that you'd find anywhere. It is rustic and primitive and remote. It's right in the heart of the Three Sisters Mountains in the Cascades at about fifty-five hundred feet in elevation. It's directly west of Bend on Century Drive. To get there you go up past the Mount Bachelor ski area and past Dutchman Flat and Todd Lake junction. Just before Elk Lake is Quinn Meadows Horse Camp. You have to call the Forest Service to get a reservation and a spot to camp.

The only structures in Quinn Meadows Horse Camp are the designated camps. They are numbered and each has a big heavy picnic table with either a tie stall or a twelve-foot corral for one horse. A gravel road makes a circle. The camp sits right on the edge of a big meadow. A lot of wildlife graze in the meadow. Elk are in the meadow every night in the summer, every single night. Once in awhile one would get confused and we'd hear him run through camp on the old dirt road.

There is no piped water. A little creek, Sink Creek, flows through camp. We got water out of Quinn Creek, which was about two hundred yards away. It flows out of hundreds of springs that come right out of the cliff, about half a mile across the meadow from the camp. The water is drinkable and ice cold.

Quinn Creek is about thirty feet wide and ranges from one to four feet deep. It flows about two miles down into Hosmer Lake, which is loaded with landlocked salmon. You can fish for these salmon with barbless hooks only. You have to turn them loose.

It is beautiful trail riding country. From Quinn Meadows you can go in any direction and ride. You can ride up into the high lakes or the low lakes basin. There are hundreds of mountain lakes in the area they call Lake Basin.

The best ride out of Quinn Meadows is back toward Mount Bachelor. You go by Goose Creek, by Wickiup Prairie, past Moraine Lake and on up into Green Lakes, then up over the shoulder of South Sister Mountain and down into Todd Lake and Todd Lake Meadow. Words cannot describe the beauty of the trip along the terrain of this trail. At least five hundred lakes are within a ten mile radius of the trail going into Green Lakes.

This is a long ride if you made the circle. We usually hauled the horses up and rode back to camp. Sometimes we rode up from Quinn Meadows to Todd Lake Meadow and had somebody meet us there with the trucks and haul the horses back.

We had an old horse camp at Todd Lake Meadow that was a horse camp simply because people with horses went there. It had all kinds of water. A nice spring came out of the hill that you could use for yourself. It is an area with outstanding riding.

Todd Lake Meadow is six thousand feet in elevation and is in the heart of the Three Sisters mountain area. Art Middleton took me into Todd Lake Meadow for the first time and I fell in love with it. Of course, I fell in love with all of the horse camps, but Todd Lake Meadow would have to be my number one favorite of all places to camp. You can still go in there with a horse.

7 The Way West at Todd Lake Meadow

In 1967 we drove in to Todd Lake Meadow to stay for two weeks. When we rolled into lower Todd Lake Meadow, here were several big semi-trucks and electric wires going everywhere. I was doggonned if they weren't making a movie. It was called "The Way West." It starred a lot of heavies: Kirk Douglas, Robert Mitchum, Richard Widmark, Lola Albright, Stubby Kaye, Sally Field.

They had tons of equipment. Semi-trucks held their electrical equipment, sound equipment, and other gear. They had brought thirteen Conestoga covered wagons from Hollywood. They were there ninety days.

We went on up to middle Todd Lake Meadow where we normally camped. I had always been a fan of western movies and here were some of my favorite actors. I made up my mind that I was going to go down and spend some time at the movie place.

At that time I had Gentlemen Jack, my big black horse who looked like a Thoroughbred but was registered as a Quarter horse. He was a good looking son of a gun, real natty. He moved out well and when I rode him, people would look around at him.

That afternoon I cleaned Jack up and saddled him. Man! He looked sharp. At that time I was riding in the sheriff's posse and we all had fancy gear. I had some of that on him—a good looking handmade roping saddle, Navajo saddle pads, a sharp-looking headstall.

The movie makers had it arranged so outsiders could not get in to the filming area. It was about four in the afternoon when I rode down to where there was a guy on a gate. Of course, all this was strange to Jack and he had his ears sharp and himself pointed straight out looking at everything. I got to talking with the gatekeeper.

I told him, "You know, I'm an old country boy up here in Oregon and I never have seen a movie made. I'd sure like to get in there and see what goes on."

He said, "I'm not supposed to let anybody in, but I heard them talking a little bit ago. They're going to quit at five. Wait a few minutes."

At four thirty he said, "You go on and ride on down there."

I headed Jack down to see where the Conestoga wagons were. They had them in a big circle like it was a fight. About that time the filming broke up and the actors and crew started walking back towards the trucks, towards me.

They had a few real Indians and about one hundred young men as extras from around the country. They had stripped them down to the waist, taken them into the makeup room and sprayed them with paint and put a wig on them. A lot of them had feathers on. By, God, they looked more like Indians than the real Indians did. There were a couple of great big Indians there. I never did know whether they were Indians or whether they were painted. They had headdresses on and were walking out.

Jack took one look at these Indians and decided he did not care much about them. By this time, I was surrounded by people walking by us. I thought, good Lord, it would be just my luck for me to have a little rodeo. But even though Jack was watching everything carefully, I did not have trouble controlling him.

Kirk Douglas walked along behind the Indians. He was talking earnestly to the actress, Katherine Justice. We got to within twenty feet from Kirk Douglas. He looked up and stopped talking as they walked by me. I waved and said, "Hello."

He said, "Hi, there," as I rode by. He was looking at Jack. You could tell he liked what he saw.

To me, it's a thrill to ride a good looking horse that's got a lot of zip to him, yet well trained to where you can handle him. I was so proud of that horse, riding in there.

I made friends quickly simply because of Jack. I saw a guy on horseback eye me as I rode up. I stopped beside him.

He said, "I like your horse."

I said, "Well, thanks, I do, too." I said, "That's not a bad looking one you're on."

He said, "Yeah, this one has been in a lot of these movies."

It was a buckskin horse, the one that Robert Mitchum rode in the movie. It turned out he was the head wrangler, Corky Randal. They had brought about forty horses from Hollywood plus about twenty oxen.

Don Carlton on Gentleman Jack.

All the horses that were used close to the camera were Hollywood horses. They brought so many because they wanted what they called "nondescript" horses. They didn't want a horse with a clipped mane or even a bridle path in the mane because that dates them.

It was now about five o'clock and the crew was getting ready to go back to Bend. They went back to town at night and came back in the morning.

Corky wanted to know what we were doing up there. I told

him the same thing I had told the gatekeeper. I said, "I'm just an old country boy. I've never seen a movie made. I'd sure like to watch some of this."

He said, "Well, I'll tell you what you do. Tomorrow morning about seven, not any later than that and maybe a little before, you ride your horse right on in here like you owned the place. Come on down here and we'll fix a place where you can tie him. You can spend the day.

"Hell, that'll be all right," he said. "Just don't get in the way of production. That's really why they're so particular. They shoot only one or two scenes a day. We average about one minute every day of finished film. We might take five hours worth, but by the time it's cut and ready for production, it won't be more, on the average, than a minute a day."

He told me, "If they're filming, whatever you do, don't make any noise. If you have to cough, swallow it. If you make noises, that's when they get unhappy. If something happens and that's the best take, then it's ruined. Just be careful."

The rest of the guys were going to go on a ride the next day. I said, "No, I'm going to go down and see that movie."

The next morning I was there at six thirty. I had Jack all shined up. I told the guy on the gate that Corky sent me. He said, "Good, go ahead, go on in."

I tied Jack where the major bunch of horses were. I didn't tie him with the other horses; they had a place where I could tie separately.

I went to where they were making the movie. I was thrilled.

The first guy I saw was Jack Elam. He was the preacher in the movie. I got to talking with him. I told him, "Hey, this is my first shot at this."

He said, "Well, just stay out of the way."

I talked to Robert Mitchum. He was easy to get acquainted with and treated me very well.

Mitchum told me, "Everybody thinks that this is such a glamorous way to make a living. You know, this is the most boring thing in this whole world. You just watch. We'll be here all day long and we'll be shooting this one scene, and those cameras won't be rolling probably more than thirty minutes this whole day, if that much. But," he said, "everything has to be just right."

It was a bright summer day with plenty of sunshine. There wasn't a cloud in the sky. Yet they had lights and reflectors all around the scene. When they took that picture, there were no shadows. Even though a man had a cowboy hat on, you could see his whole face. They had something like a big white sheet that would be facing the sun, but would reflect light back so everything was lit.

Everything had to be perfect. They had trouble with vapor trails left in the sky by jets. They couldn't film with the trails in the background. They couldn't film even the slightest look of a road.

I was amazed at the efficiency. The people who were taking care of horses were experts at what they were doing. I did not see one prima donna, including the stars.

When that director said, come on, let 'em roll, it's time to go, or whatever, nobody got out of line.

It was like Mitchum said. They waited and waited and waited and waited, then they shot a scene. Then somebody said, "I don't think that's right."

So they went back and discussed it and changed it a little. Then they shot the scene over again.

The filming the first day I was in there was of the wagon train. Robert Mitchum was the guide on the wagon train and Kirk Douglas was the wagonmaster. Richard Widmark was one of the leading members of the wagon train. One of the people in the wagon train had killed an Indian boy.

The chief had ridden up. Here were all these Indians behind him, but back about fifty feet. They were just coming over the brow of a big hill, about a hundred Indians, all in single file, and all on horseback. Their Indian chief was dressed in his Indian splendor and finery, with beautiful feathers, sitting proudly on his big paint horse. It sent a chill up my back.

The chief also had his dead son on another small paint horse, more of a pony size, probably thirteen and a half hands. The Indian boy was about thirteen years old.

They had a framework that looked very Indian. The Indian boy was sitting on the horse, tied to the framework, which was cinched to the horse.

Robert Mitchum was the go-between in the conversation between Kirk Douglas and the Indian chief. The Indian chief was talking and Kirk Douglas said, "What does he say?"

Mitchum said, "He says that while they want no blood of ours, of the wagon train, however, he does want the man who killed his son."

Mitchum says, "Hold it!"

Everything stopped. He said, "Would an Indian say 'however'? Good, Lord, that doesn't sound right."

So they talked it over. I think they finally decided to leave that in. They filmed that scene all day. They filmed it several times, then they stopped and shoved the lights around, changing the light angles, and worked at it a little differently.

It got to be warm that day and it was supposed to be winter time. Some of the them were dressed in heavy clothes. The Indian kid, tied to the framework could move his arms and hands but he was supposedly dead, sitting upright and tied to the horse. Pretty soon the kid leaned down and whispered to the wrangler who was in the background helping tend the horses.

The wrangler said, "Hold it. The kid's gotta go."

They untied the kid from the top of the pony and took him around behind one of the wagons. He had been sitting there too long and just couldn't hold it any longer. They got him back in the contraption and began filming some more.

Then something happened and the kid's pony spooked, broke loose from the Indian chief who was holding the lead rope, and ran back to the corrals where all the horses were kept. It was about three hundred yards away.

It scared everybody. It could have been a terrible accident. The kid couldn't get off. He was tied to the pony. They had taken a lot of precautions, but it was just one of those things that shows that accidents can happen at almost any time, especially with horses.

Later that day I was talking to Robert Mitchum. He called me, "sheriff." I said, "Hey, I'm not sheriff."

He said, "Well what is this thing on your belt buckle?"

I explained to Mitchum. It was a sterling silver belt buckle that the posse gave to retiring captains. In the middle was a little gold star that said "Sheriff" on it. Then in smaller letters on top, it said, "Captain of the Multnomah County Sheriff's Posse 1964." But what it showed from a distance was "Sheriff."

He said, "Everybody in here thinks you're the sheriff. Hell, just keep your mouth shut. You're doing all right." He said, "I'll tell you what I'd do. For one thing, I'd take off those spurs. If you walk around and they're jingling while they're filming, they won't like that." He said, "Just stay behind the camera, keep your mouth shut and take those spurs off."

He gave me some good advice there.

Jack Elam and Kirk Douglas were very friendly. I took pictures of all of them. When I first got to Kirk Douglas, I said, "Hey, Kirk, let me take a picture. He drew his gun and posed for the picture. I thanked him.

Richard Widmark wouldn't talk to anybody. He seemed to be a very serious actor and kind of a loner. I took one picture of him that depicted that feeling.

He was in a group of people with actresses and actors every place. But he was sitting out alone slouched down in a chair, his legs crossed, and his chin in his hands watching what was going

Robert Mitchum and Richard Widmark rest during shooting of The Way West *in 1967 at Todd Meadows near Bend, Oregon.*

on. No one was within twenty feet of him, I never felt like he wanted me to say anything to him, and he sure as heck didn't say anything to me. While he wasn't impolite, he was very aloof.

I talked to Stubby Kaye and John Mitchum, Robert Mitchum's brother. Joe Douglas, Kirk's son, was there working on the sound effects. I was impressed with the special effects people. If you gave them a little time, very little, they could build anything. They were ingenious.

The movie crew worked six days a week. They didn't work on Sunday, but I was down there. They were shoeing the oxen. That's a job not many people in this world know how to do.

One morning Grace woke me and said, "Look out the front window." We were camped in the middle of Todd Lake Meadow and were asleep in our bed in the cabover part of our camper. I looked out the front window and was transferred back in time about one hundred years.

It was about five in the morning, just getting daylight, and here goes the wagon train heading up for the day's filming. Some were pulled by ox teams, some by mules, some by horses. Everyone was in costume. You could see it as it must have looked one hundred years ago. Here was a wagon train headed for Oregon.

Of course, I shucked out of there and got something to eat real quick and saddled up Jack. Guy Beck and I headed up to see what was going on that day.

Sally Field was the young girl on the trip. She was supposed to be pregnant. The guy that shot the Indian kid was her lover, so she was going to commit suicide. She was supposed to jump off a cliff as the wagon went by a high point. They had the cameras set up there.

I rode Jack right up on the other side. It was a little canyon and I wasn't over forty feet away from where she was to jump. Corky's son, who was about fourteen years old, doubled for Sally Field.

He rode up and jumped. Oh, man! It gave me a thrill. He jumped head first right into a bunch of rocks down in this canyon. But the rocks were sponge rubber. They looked for all the world like rocks.

He stood up. It hadn't hurt him at all. They dusted him off. He did that two or three times so they got a good shot of it. I think that was the whole filming that day.

Andrew, the son of the old actor, Victor McLaglen, was the

director of this movie. Believe me, he was in charge. What he wanted, he got, and there was no argument.

Harry Carey, Jr., was also in that movie. Harry Carey, Jr., of course, is the son of famous Harry Carey, an old-time western cowboy actor. Harry Carey, Jr., was the same type of actor. He has been in many of John Wayne's films.

Everyone was working hand-in-hand to make a good movie. I wound up with much respect for everybody I saw working on that film.

Here is something to illustrate how much trouble they took to get everything exactly right. The wagon train was supposed to be going across snowfields in high country in the winter time. They went up on Mount Bachelor in the Three Sisters Mountains behind Bend. They pulled three or four of these big Conestoga wagons up there with a D-8 Caterpillar. They had to have a special OK from the Forest Service, and they had to return everything just like it was, get rid of the tracks made by the D-8.

It took them a day to get set up. As I remember, they were just above the top of the main ski lift. The D-8 Caterpillar pulled those wagons straight up the mountainside. They were big regular Conestoga wagons, the exact replicas of the old-timers.

The next day they filmed. Guy Beck, Denny Wells and I rode up to where they were going to film. Mount Bachelor is one of the best ski areas in the Northwest and it is skied about nine months out of the year. We had to hit it crossways and switchback going up there because it was so steep. We crossed back and forth under the ski lift as we made our way up.

The actors and all of the crew were riding the ski lift up. Kirk Douglas and Jack Elam and all the actors waved at us.

Pretty soon we looked up and here comes Robert Mitchum riding up on the ski lift. When we saw him he was pretty high up. He looked down at us and called out, "Which way did they go?" like we were the sheriff's posse looking for somebody. He was like that, very friendly and a lot of fun.

They filmed up there for two or three days. It was the part where they had a disturbance between the wagonmaster and one of the wagon train members. There was a big fight between Kirk Douglas and, as I remember, Richard Widmark. We did not get to see that. They had it arranged where we couldn't get up to it.

One day they were going to film on Dutchman Flat. It lies between Mount Bachelor and lower Todd Lake Meadow where we were camped. Guy, Denny and I were going to ride over there early that morning. We rode from camp across country about a mile. We broke into Dutchman Flat and, again, it took us back one hundred years.

Here was the whole wagon train coming across Dutchman Flat and they were filming, and here we walked right into the middle of it on the far end. Three guys rode out there on their horses and waved us off. We, of course, dove back into the brush and rode around. Nobody ever said anything to us. That's the only time we interfered with the movie making.

I spent my two weeks' vacation right there watching them make that movie. I used all the film I had brought up for my whole vacation taking pictures of everybody in there.

Camping with horses is something you have to want to do. You can't simply take a horse on a camping trip, hang him in a tree and forget him until you're ready to ride again.

You have to be there to take care of him. He has to be fed. He needs to move around. You can tie him and leave him all night, but he needs exercise during the day. Sometimes the horse gets to nuzzling his hay and pushes it farther than he can reach. You need to be close to him, so you can kick that hay up to where he can clean it up.

The first thing you have to do is put up a picket line. The Forest Service insists that you not tie a horse to a tree—and for good reason. A horse's instinct is to paw down to grass. When horses run in the wild or on ranges, they paw through snow to grass to get enough to live on.

The trouble comes along about feeding time in camp. Usually several groups are in camp and not everyone feeds his horse at the same time. So someone feeds his horse and your horse sees it. He's hungry and he wants his feed, so he starts to paw. I have seen horses paw two-foot deep holes at the base of trees. They dig out the roots, which kills the tree.

That pawing is why the Forest Service is adamant about not tying a horse to a tree, no matter where you are.

I carried plenty of rope to tie between two trees to make a picket line from twelve to sixteen feet long. Before I tied the rope to the tree, I slid a cinch ring without a cinch on it over the rope, then fastened the ends of the rope to each tree. I tied my horse to the cinch ring. The ring slid along the rope and gave the horse the freedom to walk back and forth along the picket line.

Horses usually stay in the middle of the picket line unless they are relieving themselves. Most horses will move to the far end of the picket line so they defecate and urinate as far away from their feed as they can.

If you put up a picket line breast high, a horse will usually go under it. So you might as well put it six feet high, which I did. I tied the halter rope to the picket line so it was long enough that the horse could just reach the ground with its muzzle, but not long enough that the rope was going to lie on the ground where he could get a foot over it. It takes awhile to learn how long to tie the halter rope.

If part of the halter rope is lying on the ground, the horse is eventually going to put a front foot over that rope. Then, unless he is pretty well broke, when he backs up and that rope comes up under his leg, he'll spook and maybe throw himself and get hurt. A horse that isn't used to a rope under his legs can fight it until he kills himself.

Anyone who has horses should know how to tie a bowline knot. You use it often on picket lines and in other ways. It does not slip and it's easy to untie.

A horse is an outdoor animal. He can withstand just about anything—rain, snow or cold, although he prefers to get out of the wind. A horse stays warm when he is outside by moving around. If he gets cold, he runs to warm himself.

I don't mind seeing a horse out in the weather. Many times I have seen a horse leave a warm stall and go out and back up to the rain, evidently because it feels good to him. But I don't like to tie a horse out in bad weather where he can't move around and keep himself warm.

When I was in camp, my horse was tied most of the time, so I carried a tarp that I could string up between two trees and make a shelter for him. Even though there might not be a cloud in the sky, when I made camp, I always put up my tarp.

A tarp shelter has to be fairly high to get over a horse. I am not one who can shinny up a tree where there aren't any low branches, so I worked out a system. I used a four-ounce lead fishing sinker. I tied a stout nylon string to that, ten feet long. I looked for a branch eight or ten feet off the ground, and threw that sinker over that branch. Then I tied the nylon string to the end of my rope in a slip knot, and pulled the rope over the branch with the nylon string. I tied the rope off to the tree and that gave me an anchor up high for one end of the tarp.

I ran that rope between two trees and made that rope the

Ed Quigley, western artist, and Reub Long, co-author of The Oregon Desert, *at the 1969 Skyline Trail Riders outing at Park Meadow in the Three Sisters Wilderness.*

centerpiece of the tarp and then strung the tarp out on both sides. This always worked well. I got kidded a lot about it, but my horse shelter always paid off.

Bob Eastman, Bob Spring, Art Middleton and I belonged to Skyline Trail Riders. The group was headquartered in Bend, Oregon. We had members from all over the Western states, and maybe some from the East. There used to be about a hundred of us.

The big event of the Skyline Trail Riders was a four-day trail ride about the second week of August every year. At one particular ride we had about sixty horses and riders. We hauled into the Diamond Peak Wilderness area.

Diamond Peak Wilderness lies behind Crescent Lake in the Cascade Mountains. It is about six thousand feet in elevation. When we drove in there, it was raining with some big snowflakes intermixed. It was cold and it was wet.

We couldn't take a trailer or a camper. We had to sleep in a tent. So Bob and I put up our tent and our cots. Then we each put up tarp "barns" so our horses had a dry place to stay.

It rained almost the entire four days we were there. Bob and I rode every day. By the third day, though, some people couldn't ride because their horses had sore backs. Their horses had been tied out all night on the picket line in the rain. They had to put their saddles on wet backs. When a wet back heats up, it gets very sore.

On the fourth day, Bob and I were the only riders out of sixty who could put a saddle on our horses. The others were just too sore. It was the tarp barns that made the ride enjoyable for our horses and for us.

I have taken a lot of kidding over that tarp, but I wouldn't trade it for anything.

Hobbles are another item that make camping with a horse enjoyable. If you are out riding and stop for lunch or something, you don't want to have to hang on to your horse. I always had a horse that I could tie for as long as I needed to. If he was prone to paw, I would hobble him and tie him. I don't think I ever left the barn or left camp without a pair of hobbles hanging from the saddle.

When I stopped for lunch, I liked to hobble my horse, pull his bridle off if there was grass around, and let him relax and feed. If I was going to be there for some time, I pulled off the saddle, too. It helped to air his back. I rubbed his back a little after I pulled off the saddle. I could see by the way he stretched into the rub that it felt good.

The lightest hobbles to carry are plain Utah hobbles, which consist of a leather strap with a buckle on one end and two rings during the length of it. You put one end of the leather strap around the horse's front leg and run it through one of the rings. Snug it up around his leg, run it through the other ring and around the other leg and buckle it. This makes it tight so he can't pull his hoof through the hobbles.

I carried my Utah hobbles in the slot in the saddle skirting that the rear flank cinch would go through. I just left them there. The only time they ever came off is when they were on the horse's feet.

I also carried a pair of large chain hobbles to use in camp. They were too big to carry on the saddle. Mine were made with heavy leather straps on each end, which were lined with sheepskin, then a chain link between. Each leather strap buckled around each front leg. I could hear that chain rattling, which helped to locate my horse.

Johnny Adair used another type of hobbles that worked well. It was a light chain, about the weight you would use around a dog's neck, about fifteen or eighteen inches long, with a snap on each end. Johnny simply snapped that chain around each front

Czech Cowboy grazing with fleece-lined hobbles.

ankle of his horse, which left about ten inches of chain between the legs.

The first time I saw it, I thought, gee whiz, that chain will tear up a horse, rough up his front legs. But it didn't. I never saw a horse hurt himself with hobbles like that. I guess the hardness of the chain cuts into his ankles if he pulls against it and stops him before he gets cut.

You can make a pair of them for probably less than two dollars, whereas a good pair of Utah hobbles costs a good deal more. The leather hobbles with a chain in the middle cost even more.

Wil Howe, a well-known horse trainer and friend of mine, designed his own hobbles for training and all-around purposes. They consist of two heavy-duty leather straps double stitched together with nylon in between. They are strong and unbreakable.

It's easy to teach a sensible horse how to handle hobbles. You can do it abruptly: put a halter with a long halter shank on the horse, hobble him, and turn him loose. He will fight the hobbles a bit and maybe fall once or twice. So start him off in a soft place— a grassy area or arena where there are lots of shavings. He will learn quickly, but that's doing it the hard way for the horse.

I used the one-legged hobble to teach a horse to hobble. The hobble is a leather strap with a D-ring on it, lined with sheepskin. You strap it on one front ankle. I put it on the left leg first, although you could put it on either one. Put a lead rope in the D-ring.

The horse has a halter on with a lead shank on it so you control him simultaneously with the lead shank and the one-legged hobble rope. Put pressure on the lead rope that is snapped onto the D-ring on the hobble. It takes a horse just a few minutes to get used to the pressure on his front foot. At that point, unsnap the lead shank from the halter and control him with just the lead tied to the left front foot.

Start the horse in a grassy area. The grass keeps his mind off what you are doing. He eats the grass and pretty soon he is leaning over and his foot is sticking out leaning against your pressure. Then the foot is in the air as he leans over and reaches for fresher grass.

After he's used to it on that foot, put the hobble on the other front foot and snap the lead rope on it. He gets used to the hobble so fast that you can usually do the training within one hour.

After he gets used to having each front foot tied separately, take the one-legged hobble off and put on the pair of hobbles. As a rule, the horse will stumble a time or two and take short steps or hop a bit, but he won't fight the hobbles.

Another method to break a horse to hobbles is to tie an old tire or log on the end of a twenty-foot rope attached to the D-ring on the one-legged hobble. The horse is not going to get hurt if you work with him a little bit to start him. He will drag that tire around and keep reaching for the fresher grass. He won't run off.

You also can put about a five-foot chain on a one-legged hobble and let a horse drag that. The horse is always stepping on that chain with a hind foot and it fouls him to keep him from running.

Usually, if you have another horse in camp, the hobbled horse is not going to run off anyway. If you're out alone, use the tire or stump or log to teach him.

Many times a horse gets to where he can move around with hobbles almost as good as without them. Some horses can come close to a good canter wearing hobbles. Most won't unless something scares them, such as other horses coming into camp or something like that. Hobbles do handicap the horse, especially if the halter has a rope trailing. A sure way of keeping a horse close is to tie the lead rope from his halter to the hobbles, known as squaw tying. The horse can't get his head high enough to run.

If there was grass in camp, we always hobbled a few of the horses and turned them out. If there wasn't grass, they would try to find some and might take off. We always kept a horse in camp in case something spooked the others and they got away. When I hobbled a horse, it was where I had an eye on him. I never lost a horse.

I never hobbled a horse and turned him out on grass all night. As far as I know, and I have been on many campouts, there is no surefire way of keeping a horse close to camp when you're sleeping unless you tie him.

I have been on trips where we had pack horses and made a different camp every night. A friend of mine, Lawton McDaniel who lived all of his life in Joseph, Oregon, in the beautiful Wallowa Mountains, was an outdoorsman from way back. He always had some pack mules and horses at his cabin on Bear Creek.

Lawton knew the mountains and always stopped where there was a meadow. Some of the grass up there is just outstanding, such as elk sedge. It has little bits of grain on the end of it and it is good feed. A horse can fill up quickly.

Lawton always put a bell on the lead mare, the one that was

Lawton McDaniel and his pack string in the Wallowa Mountains.

usually in charge. He would have four pack mules and a couple of saddle horses. He used only chain hobbles.

He turned all of the stock loose at night except one. He knew where the horses were because he could hear the bell. If the bell started getting faint, he would hop on the horse and go after them.

Lawton didn't sleep with us. He went back on the trail to a narrow place and slept right next to that trail. Every once in awhile, around two o'clock in the morning that bell would wake him. His pack string was on the way home. And every once in awhile they would get by him and he would have to ride after them.

Stan Maves, Lawton McDaniel and Art Middleton in the Wallowa Mountains, 1968.

_____

I was asked to judge a competitive trail ride that a Tennessee
Walking Horse club held for its members. About twenty-five people
took part. The ride went over an eight-mile course. The horses
were normally shown and ridden in the arena. I didn't realize that
they hadn't been outside much. I assumed they were used to the
trail and were fair trail horses.

I judged the trail ride by giving one hundred points to every
rider at the start of the ride. Then I deducted points for errors
that were made along the trail. From the beginning it was obvious
that every horse in this group was not used to the trail.

One of the most glaring errors was one horse crowding the
horse in front. A good trail rider does not let his horse walk right
behind another horse. So I deducted for that.

I deducted for poor horse manners. This included how the
horse acted if everyone on the trail stopped. Was the horse eager
to go, throwing his head, dropping his head, turning around on
the trail? Was he hard to handle? Or did he stand quietly and wait
for his master to command him to go.

One rider's horse got so excited it started rearing up and
eventually went over backwards with the rider. The rider, luckily,
knew enough to slip to one side and wasn't hurt. He got back up
on the horse. That horse was not trained for trail riding.

I also judged how the horse acted when the rider was on the
ground, for instance, at the lunch stop. Did the horse stand quietly,
or did the rider have to hold the horse while he was eating lunch
and not be able to sit down because the horse was not easily
controlled on the ground.

I looked for good control of the horse in other ways. Say the
horse and rider approached a stream. The horse looked at it. Maybe
he was a little doubtful of it. Maybe he couldn't see the bottom.
Maybe the water was fast.

If the horse hesitated and looked at the water, I did not dock points. It's good for a horse to look at what he's doing, notice where he's going. But when that rider touched that horse with the spurs, the horse should have confidence in the rider and go through the water.

If the pair were there for fifteen minutes before the rider got the horse into the water, the horse had not been trained to do what the rider was asking it to do. I deducted for the delay. Some of the horses would not cross the creek.

There was not a good trail horse in the entire group. These horses, for the most part, had been trained for their walking ability, their showmanship in the show ring, not for trail riding.

This experience shows just some of the problems in handling horses on the trail. When you are out in the hills, it doesn't take long to pick out the people and horses you like to ride with and the people and horses you would just as soon not ride with.

I have ridden with people who had horses that jigged or trotted. So the riders crowded the horse in front to slow their own horses down to a walk. A good trail horse and a good trail rider should never crowd the horse in front. Rather, they should stay about eight or ten feet behind the horse ahead. This is especially important in steep country and heavily wooded country like western Oregon.

I have ridden with people who have ridden right on my horse's tail in a bad place in the trail. I guess it made them feel safe. If we had been going downhill and my horse had stumbled and fallen, that someone and their horse who was right smack behind me would have been right on top of me or my horse.

If maybe three or four riders had been riding behind the horse that was in trouble, all of them jammed up nose to tail, everyone would be in trouble. If it happened on a steep trail and maybe on a switchback with steep sides on it, it's going to be bad trouble.

I have seen some big problems on some steep bad trails. I've seen horses slip crossing the shale slide on the Horseshoe Ridge trail. I have seen horses step in a hole. I have seen the side of the trail give way beneath the horse.

Yet, many people who trail ride do not give this a second thought. I do not plan to ride with that kind of rider very often. If they continue to press me on the trail, following nose to tail, I simply will not ride with them.

On a Ramona Falls ride, we had an accident that pointed up

the importance of being with a group of trail-smart riders. As a rule, the group I rode with numbered about five or six, sometimes seven or eight.

Every now and then a horsemen's group would have a steak fry or cowboy breakfast up at Frank Riley Horse Camp. It was during one of these outings, where there were a lot of riders and we were in a large group, that the accident happened.

We went around Ramona Falls, then came back and crossed Ramona Creek where a small bridge crosses it. It's a regular Forest Service bridge, about four feet wide and twenty feet long with no railing. It's made strong enough to hold a horse.

You can ford the creek, but many times a fellow would take his horse across the bridge to get the horse used to it. A horse cannot be used to too many things. A horse has a terrific memory. Once he becomes confident in one thing and realizes that his rider is not going to put him into trouble, the better the horse becomes. So, many times a rider would ride across the little bridge rather than ford the creek.

We were at that bridge on our way back from Ramona Falls. Guy Beck was in front of me. In front of him was a long string of riders. About the time Guy's horse stepped up on that bridge, somebody way up in front stopped, somebody who was not thinking very well. When that line of riders stopped, it was like a freight train stopping. Everyone bumped into the rider in front until the line was tight. Guy had left plenty of room between himself and the fellow ahead. So when the horse ahead of Guy stopped just off the bridge on the other side, it caught Guy and his horse square in the middle of the bridge.

I was behind far enough to where I could check my horse before I got onto the bridge. If I had been following right on his tail, there would have been two of us out in the middle of that bridge and two of us in trouble.

The bridge was too narrow to back up a horse. Guy hollered out, "Hey somebody up there, let's get moving. I'm on this bridge."

We were there for probably thirty seconds and Guy's horse got a little antsy, wanting to move on and get off that bridge. He stepped off the bridge with his left hind foot. The bridge was about six feet above the stream, and Guy and his horse went sideways off that bridge. Guy wound up under the horse. He was riding a big black Quarter horse named Mose that weighed about twelve hundred pounds.

I thought Guy was seriously hurt or even killed. We got the horse off him. Guy was wet from his hips down and was really hurting in his chest. We later found out he had several broken ribs. The horse was uninjured.

Guy couldn't get back on his horse and we were about a mile or so from the Muddy Fork crossing. I stayed with Guy and led his horse. He walked down to the Muddy Fork where a foot bridge crosses the river. Horses can't go over it because there are steps on it that rise about ten feet.

I rode my horse and led his horse across the stream. Someone had ridden on ahead and one of our other friends, Myrtha Middleton, came up with her car. They loaded Guy into it and took him into the hospital. He came back to camp later that evening. He was really hurting from his broken ribs. It took him a couple of months to heal.

A lot of people who ride just don't understand the hows and whys of trail etiquette. That's why I'm leery about riding with inexperienced people in the mountains. They can put you in trouble just as quick as Guy Beck got in trouble there.

Someone thoughtlessly got off their horse, stopped to tighten their saddle or give their horse a drink of water. This one thoughtless move could have cost Guy his life.

Guy's accident also shows the importance of being able to handle the rear end of a horse. You do this by teaching a horse to sidepass.

I bought a horse that didn't sidepass. After I bought him, the next issue of the *Western Horseman* magazine carried an article on how to make a horse sidepass. Following the instructions, this is what I did.

Step 1. I tied my horse to a fence, which was perpendicular to him. I stood on the ground, took my spur and touched him on the left side just behind the cinch, where my spur would touch him when I was riding. I kept pressing and said, "gate." My horse would look at me. Pretty soon he stepped over. I stopped and petted him on the neck. When he was moving away well from the spur on the left side, I went around and worked him from the right side.

Step 2. I got in the saddle and put my horse's right side up against the fence. With one hand on both reins, I tilted his mouth slightly to the left and touched him with my right spur. I said, "gate." I didn't let him move forward or backward. This was awkward at first. I then reversed him, working on the right side.

Guy Beck and Mose at Frank Riley Horse Camp, 1964.

My horse learned quickly, moving both to the left and to the right using this technique.

Step 3. I took my horse into a level place without a fence. I asked him to move to the right and to the left without moving forward or backward.

This takes patience. But if you do it properly, the horse learns very quickly. I spent several days completing these three steps.

Once the horse is trained, you can sidepass him anywhere you want to go. If you are on a steep trail, you can control his rear end as well as his front. If the high side of the trail is on the right and the low side is on the left, many times that horse's left rear foot is walking right on the edge of that trail. If he has learned to sidepass, all you have to do is give him a light right rein and tap him with your left spur and he'll bring his hindquarters back on the trail. You can control his back end with your legs as well as you control his front end with the bridle.

Suppose you are on a steep trail where it's hard to turn around such as a timber downfall on the trail with no way around. It's too steep to turn around. You can back your horse almost as far as you want because you can steer his rear end with the sidepass. When you get to a wide place, just turn his back end up the hill around his front feet. Sidepassing is one of the most essential maneuvers on any well mannered horse.

Once you've ridden a good horse that you can sidepass, pull his hips all around his front feet—both ways—with his front feet not moving, you can't stand to ride a horse you can't control.

Many times you find people who are riding horses that are very slow walkers. The riders have not learned how to make the horses walk fast. If you get behind a rider like that, you see the rider drop behind and drop behind until he is twenty or thirty feet behind. Then he kicks his horse and trots to catch up with the horses in front of him. This shakes up every horse in the bunch, especially the ones following him. Then the rider and horse start falling behind again. They fall behind another twenty or thirty feet, then the rider kicks the horse, trots and catches up.

If that's the way that rider wants to ride, he should be on the end of the procession. There he is the least amount of bother to the other riders.

There is another side to that trotting and catching up. Sometimes you get a leader who wants to show everybody how fast his horse can walk. If he kicks that horse to really stepping out and his horse walks faster than the average horse, then the fault lies with that leader.

Many horses, when they get too far behind, get to jigging and dancing all over the trail. It causes a real mess. A good trail ride leader establishes a pace that is comfortable for most horses on the ride and holds that pace.

Now and then you find a horse that absolutely plods along. It isn't the horse's fault. All horses can be taught to walk fairly fast.

You cannot set a trail ride to make that horse comfortable because he is just going too slow. The average horse has been trained to cover ground when he walks. The slow-walking horse does not belong on a trail ride with experienced and good traveling horses. If the rider of that slow horse wants to go, he should get in the back end and avoid the middle of the string where he fouls up everyone.

Another common mistake you find in a large group of riders is for a rider to gallop a horse up behind another horse when the other rider does not realize the horse is coming up behind. It excites the horse he is running up on and can cause a serious accident.

Galloping or running a horse around people who are standing still or walking can cause accidents. All horses like to run, especially if they hear another horse running.

Any time you are horseback and around other horses, unless everyone there knows you are going to kick out and run, you should not do it. It's bad practice and bad manners.

If you are horseback and run into a group of people and put on the brakes because you are feeling good and you want to show how good your horse can stop, it might be fine. But you might also have somebody on the ground before it's all over. This is probably one of the most flagrant mistakes made when riders are out in groups.

I had one horse, Blackie, that if I saddled him up early in the morning and went for a ride by a pasture with horses I had to hold onto him tight. The horses in the pasture, especially in the spring of the year, would get excited when we went by. They would whistle and whinny at him and soon would all be running.

Blackie would be feeling good, especially on a chilly morning. He would want to run. I had to hold on to him and make him do what I wanted him to do, not what he wanted to do. I would never let a horse run because he wanted to run. That makes the difference in riding a horse that's controlled and one that's not. The only way he was going to run is when I wanted him to run.

Yellowjacket trouble is another circumstance where I want to be with trailwise riders. As you get into the fall of the year in the Northwest, yellowjackets become a problem, especially in a dry year. If there is a wet place in the trail, the yellowjackets seem to build their nests there. The first horse goes over the nest, then the second horse, then the third.

By that time the yellowjackets are pouring out of that hole in the ground. They sting the horse that's on top of the hole. The horse in the lead gets off Scot free and maybe even the second horse. But from there on back, it's trouble.

The worst thing that can happen is for somebody to freeze on their horse. If someone up ahead stops and blocks a guy standing over the bee nest, he is in big trouble. If it's in a bad part on the trail, which I have seen happen, it can be a real experience.

I have gotten into bees many times. I know the minute a horse jumps a little bit or switches his tail or really wakes up with a start, it's more than likely bees.

Whoever makes that discovery yells, "BEES!" and everybody gets out of there quick. Even when the bees are coming up, if the guys behind ride across at a gallop, they'll probably be all right. But I have seen riders whose horses are half trying to buck, ride up two feet and freeze and block two or three people over those bees.

Guy Beck and I got into trouble with bees. I was in the lead. It was just the two of us and we had plenty of room between us. It was a very bad spot in the trail going into Eden Park, real steep on one side. Guy's horse really got stung and started to buck. For some reason or another, maybe a big nest, we both got into the bees.

I was on my horse, Gentleman Jack. Jack was alert and careful, a horse that took very good care of himself. He would not hurt himself; you could bet on that. There was a big bunch of salal brush right off the trail and we were in heavy, tall timber and on a steep hillside.

I gave Jack his head a little bit, but not enough to let him buck. He headed right into that salal brush to knock the bees off him. He wanted that brush scraping his belly and his chest to get rid of the bees.

If you ever get into bees and a horse looks like he wants to get over in the brush, let him go if you can see that he is not going to fall into anything. The brush gets rid of the bees.

But in all cases, when you get into bees, get out of there quick. If you have people behind you, do not stop ten feet up the trail. Go way on up the trail.

I have never seen bees follow a rider. They protect their nest. They sting you if you are right over that nest. Once you get by them a little, you are all right.

Horses are gregarious; they love company and company of their own kind. If you have two horses stabled and ridden together, they sometimes get so accustomed to each other that they go almost crazy when they are separated.

We have had couples on camping trips who wanted to go with us on a ride, but they had two spoiled horses. One of them would say, "I've got to stay behind Bill because my horse won't go any place himself." Usually if the horse does go someplace himself and gets behind somebody else, he is right on the tail, almost stepping on the heels of the horse in front.

If you are keeping two horses together, don't always ride together. Make it a point every time you ride to split up and get out of sight of one another several times during your ride. Take one of the horses and ride off. I don't mean when you ride with someone that you go in different directions and not join up. But separate during your ride, then join up. You can start off riding in different directions, or after you get going. If a trail splits and you can go separately for ten minutes or so, do it.

If you ride off, a horse is not going to get really nasty unless it is spoiled rotten. He will throw a tantrum the first time. He will balk and won't go and so forth. Ride separately until the horse gets through whinnying and throwing a temper tantrum. You simply have to be in charge and make him go. Ride in different directions and you soon find you have a horse with which you are comfortable when you are around other horses.

Train them right. Horses are so easy to train and they are so susceptible to good training that it's a shame to see them spoiled. A good horse knows he must do what you want. A horse is not a good horse unless you are the master. If he is the master, he is in charge.

If you go trail riding enough with twenty or more horses, you are going to see almost all of the things I have mentioned. So, when you go trail riding, pick your riding companions.

I have known one man ever since I have been in the Portland area. He is a good horseman; he is a good rider. He is a poor camper and a poor trail companion. He just doesn't use his head when he's on a trail with a horse. He has done some of the dumbest things in the world. Occasionally, I would get stuck in a group with him, but not for long.

The group I rode with were a pleasure to ride with. Everyone was a good horseman and understood how to take care of himself and his horse in the mountains, on the trails and in camp.

Riding partners: Marlin Hamilton, Guy Beck, Don Carlton, Sid Murray and Whitey Ford at Frank Riley Horse Camp, 1963.

In 1968 I decided the boat was in the way and I missed having my horse on my own place. So we decided to sell our place and move to acreage in Wilsonville, which at that time was in the country. Around this time I bought Rusty.

Lyle Boyce had about forty acres in La Center, Washington, and always had a few horses around. He had an eye for well built, big horses. Lyle had bought a King ranch-bred Quarter horse at a Quarter horse sale as a yearling. His registered name was Rusty Mia. Lyle had planned to keep him as a stallion, but he was so mean that he castrated him and made a gelding out of him. In a week's time, Rusty had settled down. In two or three weeks' time, he had lost all the meanness and was a trainable horse.

Denny Wells had done a lot of the training on Rusty so he had a good rein on him and was well started. Lyle decided to sell Rusty and advertised him in the paper. I had seen the horse and really liked him. Denny called me and told me that Lyle was selling that Rusty horse.

I called Lyle who said Rusty was over at Bill Robbins' place. Bill was another old cowboy who had horses. I drove to Bill's and took my saddle with me. I put the saddle on Rusty and led him around. Bill was not too sure whether I was going to get along with Rusty, who was an active, young horse.

I got on him and rode him out the gate and down the road. It was a blacktop road, which I did not like to be on with a new, young horse, but it was the only place I could ride. As I came out of the gate, Rusty was tight as a bowstring. He was walking just like he was on eggs.

I would lay that rein on his neck and he would spin right around. I knew he could have bucked me over the highest tree there, but I knew that I was going to buy him. So I made an offer to Bill.

Bill said, "No, I want such and such for him. He's too good a horse."

I was afraid somebody else would buy him, so I wrote him a check. I had gone over there in my pickup with a horse van on it. I dropped the tailgate, loaded Rusty and took him home. Rusty was four years old when I got him and he turned out to be the finest horse I ever owned. There is an old saying that every man deserves one good woman and one good horse. I have had both.

We had been at Wilsonville just a short time when folks stopped out front. I was working in the yard. The fellow was dressed

Don Carlton on Rusty Mia riding for Washington County Posse in 1969.

up in a suit. He came in and introduced himself as Bob Spring. He said, "Say, I'm looking at this two-and-a-half-acre lot next door to you and would like to talk to you about it."

I invited him in and we got to talking. I said, "Hey, can I pour you a drink?"

Pat Carlton holds Rusty Mia.

Bob Spring on his Quarter horse.

He laughed and said, "I just had lunch and had a drink. I put a peppermint in my mouth because I didn't want you to smell it on me."

That started a friendship that has lasted through the years. Bob and Pat Spring with their two children, Bob, Jr., and Billy, bought the place next door. They lived in a big trailer while the house was being built. Bob brought in a registered Quarter horse, a three-year-old colt by the name of Skeeter.

People moved into the house that the developer had built on two and a half acres on the other side of us. One day I looked out and here was a big, tall, slender guy over there putting up a fence so he could bring his horses in. I walked over and got acquainted.

Bob Eastman sold medicine and pharmaceutical supplies for E.R. Squibb and Sons. He had just been transferred from The Dalles with his wife, Polly, daughter, Terry, and sons, Robbie and Casey. The whole family fit right in to our family and our riding group. From that day in 1968 until today the Eastmans have remained close friends.

Bob had kept his horses at Red Harper's place in The Dalles. I helped him bring them to Wilsonville. Bob was an old Idaho ranch kid so he knew horses.

He also had a twenty-six-foot boat on a big trailer. The boat was his main recreation. The horses were for the kids. I got to talking to Bob, trying to sell him the horse-related recreation rather than the boat. He was a very susceptible listener.

I said, "Bob, you ought to sell that big boat and trailer. You'd get enough out of them to buy a nice camper or trailer and horse trailer or get a heavy duty pickup and horse van with a pull trailer."

I made arrangements for a big camp-out at Frank Riley Horse Camp on Mount Hood. I talked to all of our friends—Guy Beck, Art Middleton, Johnny Adair, Bob and Pat Spring and their family. It was not hard to talk Bob Eastman into the trip, although he had no camper or means to stay.

I told him, "Bob, you come on up. Bring a tent or sleep in your horse trailer. Plan on eating with us."

He was all for it.

I took a couple of extra days off and went up on Thursday afternoon and made camp and got ready for the rest of them. Guy and Lessie Beck were there ahead of me as were Johnny and Pearl Adair. Springs and Eastmans came in Friday afternoon.

That Friday, John Adair and Guy Beck and I went up the Horseshoe Ridge trail and came down Cast Creek trail, which is very very steep.

We were partying a bit that day, taking a few drinks. Coming down the trail Guy Beck was riding his horse Blackjack. Johnny was riding Rocky. I was riding Rusty.

Guy got overbalanced and went straight out over Blackjack's head. When he hit, the hill was so steep he rolled thirty feet. He got up kind of woozy.

Johnny took his belt off and hooked it in Guy's belt. We came down the hill with John behind Guy steering him and with me leading Blackjack.

In the meantime Bob Eastman and his sons, Casey and Robbie, drove in to camp and parked. Bob couldn't wait until we got back to camp and asked Grace which way we went. He and Robbie came up there on horseback. They met us where Cast Creek trail comes into an old fire road. Here we were, with Johnny leading Guy and me leading Guy's horse. We explained to Bob what had happened on the trail.

At that point Guy got back on Blackjack. Blackjack weighed thirteen hundred pounds. He was not that tall, but he was powerful.

He was also pretty catty for a big horse and he was young. He spooked at something.

Guy said, "Oh, you want to run, do you?"

He kicked him out down the dirt road toward camp. The trail to camp turned off the road and the road went on by. Guy didn't have any notion of turning into the trail, but Blackjack knew where that trail went. He turned into that trail at full speed. Guy went flying on down the dirt road awhile before he hit the ground. We gathered Guy up and went into camp.

Around the campfire that night, Bob Eastman told me, "You know, Don, this is my kind of living. When I get home, I'm going to run an ad and sell that boat. I'm going to get a nice big camper and a good horse trailer and we're going to enjoy this with you guys."

I knew he would. I could read it in him.

The next morning we were at the big Forest Service tables eating breakfast. Guy was sitting there holding his head. He had a bit of a hangover. Guy's wife, Lessie, came out of their camper. She had the best looking plate of breakfast you ever saw: fried potatoes, big strips of bacon, two big eggs, some biscuits and grits.

Guy looked at it and said, "Oh, I can't eat that."

Lessie looked at him and she looked at the breakfast. She said in her soft southern drawl, "Well, I'll just grind it up and put it in a bottle. You can handle it that way."

Of course, that broke up everybody. Eastman still remembers that. It was his baptism into the horse group.

Along about this time Bob Spring and I went up to the Hermiston fall sale. We were out at the corrals looking. I did not need a horse. I had Rusty and he was right in his prime at six or seven.

The bunch of colts I was looking at had been brought by Hartley Lambert from Stevensville, Montana. Lambert was a rough old cowboy. He had come in with this truckload of fourteen colts and had them in two pens. They were all pasture-bred out of his Poco Bueno-bred stallion, and were all good looking. They had come off a big ranch and none of them were halter broke.

I picked out this one colt and told Bob, "By gosh, I like that colt."

His color made him shine. It was the fall of the year so he had long hair, but he was a palomino with a good white tail and mane. He was also the biggest colt there.

An old saying says there's nothing a good little horse can do that a good big horse can't do a little better. I believe that, especially when it comes to carrying a man, doing an all day's work.

In the heat of the sale, I got excited and I'll be damned if I didn't buy that colt for two hundred and eighty dollars. I really didn't mean to. I didn't need him; I had the best saddle horse in the State of Oregon as it was. But, I got excited and the first thing I knew, I had my hand up and I owned the colt.

The next morning I paid for him and we went out to catch him. I wanted to get that colt out of the corral before the bunch had been scared around for five hours with everybody getting a colt. I told Bob, "Let's get out there first because those colts aren't halter broke and wild as deer. They're going to be hard to catch."

We went out to the corral, and, gosh, he was a big, big strong colt. I told Bob, "We're going to have to catch him, get a halter on him, and somehow or another get him out to the truck."

I had my truck with me with the horse van on it, which was enclosed.

The weather was terrible. It rained all the time we were there. There had been a thousand horses in that sale. The walkways were yellow with horse manure. With the rain, it was really wet and sloppy.

We got a halter on the colt, but in doing so, he got Bob down a couple of times. Bob had wet horse manure from his hat to his shoes. Of course, I was on the other end of the rope; I had planned things a little better.

Even after we had the halter on him, we had a hard time. I got hold of the halter rope and we put a rope behind him and got him out of the pen. Of course, the other colts were running around in the pen. This was before daylight although there were yard lights.

We got him out to the alleyway, but still had a good two hundred yards to go to get out the gate. Then we had to get him up a ramp into the back of my truck, which was four feet off the ground. The colt was scared to death. The farther away he got from the rest of the colts, the more homesick he got.

We should have sold tickets for the event; we had that many people watching us. A couple of cowboys came over and helped us and we literally carried him to the truck. I would guess he weighed four hundred pounds.

It took us probably two hours from the time we got out of that pen to get him to the truck. A seven- or eight-month-old colt is strong. By the time we got him into the van, the colt had gotten both of us down a couple of times so both of us were covered with wet horse manure.

I didn't have any horse gear with me because I had no idea at all of buying a colt. I still didn't, but here I was with one. Bob had bought a blue colt halter for me. So we had that on him and I tied him in the van on the truck. I bought a small blanket and put that on him.

I was so excited, I was beside myself. I don't think I have ever been that excited in my life. We started home. Ten minutes down the highway I had to go to the bathroom. We had our CBs so I told the guys I had to pull off. They ribbed me about being so excited. I got back in the truck and it wasn't fifteen more minutes and I had to go again. That happened three times. There is something about buying a horse at an auction that is truly exciting.

I brought the colt home and we nicknamed him Little Bit. I registered him as Poco Cisco's Kid. His sire's name was Poco Cisco and sire's sire was Poco Bueno. He was a well bred hummer. Later I called him Kid or Cisco.

When we got him home, he was a sad looking sight. Here he had lost all his brothers and sisters and nephews and cousins and was all by himself. I put him in the extra stall. He was as wild as a deer, but in a week's time I was picking up his feet and he would come.

Never in all the time I had Cisco did I go out to catch him. He always came into the stall. I would go out and put the chain up across the stall door then put his halter on. He turned his butt to me two or three times. Each time I smacked him good. He never turned his rear end to me after that. He always faced me when I went into the stall. He had excellent manners.

I knew I did not need another horse. I was working hard at a demanding job. I did well to have time to keep Rusty ridden. I kept Cisco for a year. Then I sold him to a customer, Jack Beers, for his son, Mike. They lived in Rufus, Oregon. Jack Beers ran Jack's Restaurant at Biggs Junction. Mike Beers later became a world champion team roper. Cisco turned out to be not fast enough for a good heeling horse, but he was around the Beers's stables for a long time.

In 1975, Larry and Pat Kelley moved onto Canyon Creek Road. They lived right across the road from us on two and a half acres.

At that time Pat was mostly interested in showing horses. She had a fairly good-sized Morgan gelding, Fox Den Sonadawn, that she called Sonny. He was well bred, but flighty. He did not work on the trails too well. Larry had a smaller ranch-bred Morgan gelding named Van that had been used for showing.

Eventually we took them on a horse camping trip. It was Bob and Polly Eastman, the Kelleys and us. Pat and Larry found they liked the mountains and liked to ride in them. So they decided to quit showing and use their spare time to go out on the trails. But their horses were not quiet trail riding or using type horses.

Pat's horse was good looking, but he was not a horse I liked very much. A person who didn't understand horses and looked at Sonny going down the street with a rider would think, "Man! Isn't that a pretty horse." And he was. But he was one of those whose knees were high up, ready to prance at anything. He was not a comfortable ride. I tried to nudge Pat to a good sensible Quarter horse, but Pat loved her big Morgan. She was bound and determined to make a trail horse of him.

We were on a camping trip in the Three Sisters mountain area, out of Quinn Meadows Horse Camp. Johnny Adair, Pat and Larry and I were riding back on the trails towards the lakes. Pat said, "I'm going to take a detour. You guys go on ahead. I'll catch up."

Sonny would go crazy and was pretty hard to handle when he was away from the other horses. But Pat was really working with Sonny. I sure had to give her "E" for effort. She had nerve.

She took him up the trail and he was getting shook up because he was leaving the other horses. We went on down a fairly steep hill to the bottom and waited. A few minutes later we heard her.

"Whoa, you son of a bitch, whoa."

Pat and Sonny came pouring down the hill at a dead run. Sonny's eyes were flashing he was so mad. Pat was mad, too. Johnny reached up and grabbed Sonny's bridle as they came flying by.

It seems Sonny was determined he was going to race up to us. So Pat made him walk. He got more and more agitated, throwing himself this way and that on the trail, prancing and dancing.

At one point he tried to jump between two trees that had grown out of each other in a "V" configuration. He lodged himself in there and she had to work with him to back him up. He was determined to go one way, and that was forward as fast as he could. He grabbed the bit in his mouth and headed down the trail at a dead run, making the switchbacks and missing the trees.

That wild ride still wasn't enough to persuade Pat to make a change in horses. Pat had done what a lot of people do, she had fallen in love with her horse and made a pet out of him.

The turning point came when she took Sonny on a cattle drive in 1981 at the Robertson ranch. Sonny would not settle down away from the other horses so he was pretty much useless help. When we got back to Rod Robertson's place, Pat put him in a corral by himself. He could see the other horses, but he wasn't with them. He screamed and whinnied.

Bill Robertson, Rod's dad, told Pat if she didn't get rid of that horse, the horse was going to kill her. That's when Pat decided to sell Sonny.

When we got home from that trip, Pat found someone who was looking for a Morgan that would do well in the shows and that person bought Sonny. We started looking for a horse. Pat had

Pat and Larry Kelley preparing to ride in Wilsonville's Boones Ferry Days parade on Dusty and Lucky.

a friend who raised Morgan horses, Kathryn Van Dyke. Kathy and Pat were talking and Kathy told her they had a nice looking palomino Quarter horse gelding she might like.

Pat went over and tried the horse. He seemed to be quiet and nice so she bought him and brought him home. He was six years old. His name was Dusty. Dusty was a big improvement, but he still wasn't the horse I would like to have seen her get. In the meantime Larry bought a registered Quarter horse, Lucky Spartacus, from Wamic, Oregon. He was an excellent horse.

About this time Bob Eastman was transferred to San Francisco so he sold his home next to us and left. Of course, this broke our hearts. Bob and Polly were good neighbors and dear friends.

In 1979, I had to put Rusty down. His left front knee had been injured and became completely stiff. This was tough to do. He and I had shared many happy days and camps.

After looking at many horses, I bought Blackie, a King-bred Quarter horse. His registered name was Sono Vega. He had a huge white diamond on his forehead. At night that was the only thing you could see.

He was nine years old and an excellent saddle horse. He carried me for several years in the mountains and on the desert. In 1982 Blackie developed a hip problem.

At this point I bought another excellent saddle horse by the name of Czech Cowboy. Cowboy was a sharp looking Quarter horse, a true bay with a perfect head, very good conformation and well trained. He was a smart son of a gun. He had bright, intelligent eyes and I could do anything on him as long as he knew I was going to do it.

I had been suffering through the last forty years with a back that I had injured when I was about twenty-five years old. In those days they didn't know much about treating one. The older I had gotten, the worse it had gotten.

In 1983 it got to the point that when I hobbled Cowboy, I had to get down on my hands and knees. Then I had to shinny up his leg to stand up straight again. It was painful for me to put in a long day riding. When we were through riding, I would dread getting off my horse because I was almost molded to the saddle. I had to hang onto the saddle horn and let myself down. I dreaded pulling the saddle off my horse and packing it up the ramp into my horse van.

Pat Kelley had told me if I ever wanted to sell Cowboy, she would buy him. That fall I sold him to Pat. She was tickled to death with him.

After several months, I decided to try horses again, so I bought a Thoroughbred-Morgan named Bo Jangles. Bo weighed close to thirteen hundred pounds. He was a nice, quiet, willing horse. I wasn't roper enough to do it, but if a person could rope, he could rope most anything off Bo. He was big enough to handle it.

My back problems hadn't gone away, however. So in 1984, I decided to sell Bo to Larry Kelley. Larry had had to put his good Lucky horse down due to a tumor in his nose.

At that point, I finally did get out of horses. I missed them terribly, but I spent time with my friends who had horses and I continued to go to Drewsey to help with the cattle.

Blackie, a good horse.

The best way to have a horse is on your own place where you have your own land and barn. You can do a lot of things to make it easier to care for the horse and make his life easier.

Wire fences for horses scare me, especially in a small pasture of one or two acres. Many times a horse gets his foot caught in the wire, especially if another horse is over the fence and they get to picking at each other.

If a horse gets a foot through the wire to where the wire gets back into his pastern, it's pretty hard to get the foot out, even if he is barefooted. Shoes make it even harder to get a foot out that's hung in a fence. A lot of horses have scars right above the hairline in back of the hoof. This shows where they have almost lost a foot or the use of a foot. Good judgment and electric fencing prevent that.

On my place I had two hundred yards of white wood fence. The rest was woven wire with small woven wire at the bottom so the horse couldn't get his feet through it. A wooden fence for horses is certainly the best way to go, but they are expensive and hard to maintain. Every time I painted mine, I wished I didn't have that much white fence.

In my small pasture I ran electric wire along the top of the woven wire fence and at the bottom about two feet off the ground and one foot inside. The hot wires kept the horse from getting close to the fence and the top wire kept him from reaching over and nosing or smelling or nipping the horse on the other side.

I also put electric wire on top of my wooden fence and ran a strand of electric wire in the middle so my horse could not reach through. A horse can have all the grass in the world on his side of the fence, but something on the other side always looks better to him. He will poke his head through the fence if there is a place he can do that.

A single wire one-foot inside the fence keeps the horse from getting to close to the fence. The wire on top keeps him from leaning over it. (Illustration by Woody Cooper)

A fence can't take too much of a thousand or so pound horse reaching over and pushing on it. Soon it will be at a forty-five degree angle. Eventually he'll push it over.

When I had more than one horse, I tried to keep them separate. Horses kept together on two or three acres are often skinned up. They get full of grass, get bored and start picking at each other.

When they have more room, say a pasture of five acres or more, they are less apt to pick at each other and there is more room for the picked-on horse to run without being boxed into a corner or run through a fence. I have never had more than two horses on this place. Two horses are plenty for three acres in western Oregon.

When I had two horses here, I split the pasture with a hot wire. The electric wire makes a real gentleman out of a horse and it does not hurt him. He will not get into it very many times after one experience. I know. I get into my own electric fence about twice a year. That's more than any of my horses ever has. It keeps me pretty thoughtful about where the wire is.

A horse that grows up with an electric wire fence learns to

respect all wire. If he is turned out later in his life where there is barbed wire, say on a big ranch with hundreds of miles of fences, which can't be electric or woven or board, the horse respects it and is less apt to get hung up in it.

A horse who has been leaning over a smooth wire to get fresh grass on the other side of a fence has no respect for it and he'll try the same thing on barbed wire. A horse that gets into barbed wire can get cut badly, especially if his foot hangs up in the wire.

I had a barn with two box stalls and an overhang that made a loafing shed. When I had two horses, I split the loafing shed by putting a two-by-ten board across the middle. I put up a hot wire across the top of the board if they were picking at each other. If they weren't, I didn't. Each horse had half of the loafing shed and his own stall.

I liked to let my horse run in the pasture with access to the barn. I always thought he stayed healthier. If he wanted to stand out in the rain, he could, but he had a place to get out of the rain when he wanted.

Many times I have seen my horse in the fall of the year when the first rain comes, go out and stand in it almost with a smile on his face. He would back up to the wind and rain (a horse always has his rump to the wind) and stand there. On the other hand I have seen that same horse, when the first rain hit, hietail it for the barn, get under the loafing shed and wait for it to quit.

It's important to have shelter for horses, but it just makes good sense for them to have free choice of going under shelter or outside. Most horses prefer getting behind or under a big tree during bad weather, if the pasture has a tree. Horses on western ranches run out all the time, but they have shelter they can get to.

Half of my property was open and about one acre went down into a canyon and across a creek. There were some big trees right on the edge of the hill where it started to drop down towards the creek. I could tell by looking that the horses spent the night under those trees. If we had a bad windstorm or it was real rainy and stormy, they would come up to the barn. My horses never spent much time in the barn other than what it took to eat their hay and oats.

The older I get, the more it hurts me to see a horse living in luxury in a big box stall day in and day out or even every other day. He is so bored that he is almost crazy. I have seen tether balls tied in stalls for horses to bump around to keep them from getting bored.

Boredom is where wood chewing starts. A horse won't come in and chew on the side of a two by four of a manger or other part of the stall if he can get outside. If he is outside, even if he has the pasture eaten down to where there isn't any grass, he is out there picking. His head is down. He is moving around. It keeps a horse healthy in body and mind.

Years ago, I used to bed down the stall in either sawdust or shavings and put my horse in every night. A longer time ago, I used to put him in every night and put a blanket on him. I thought I was being good to him. But a horse is an outdoor animal. I do not believe a blanket is any part of a horse's need in a normal life. Today I never blanket a horse through a regular year when I have him at his regular place.

I have found that when I did not bed down a stall with shavings or sawdust, just left the floor in dirt, that my horse would not urinate or defecate in that stall. If I gave him free choice, he went outside. I did not pick up a forkful of manure more than once a month. The stall stayed clean.

If I put sawdust or shavings in a stall, he would come from the far corner of the pasture to urinate in the stall. Horses like to urinate on sawdust or shavings and they will do most of their defecating in the stall for you to clean up. If there are no shavings in the stall, they go out and urinate on some tall grass.

There were times I did put my horse in the stall overnight. In the Northwest about half the year is mud. When we were going to haul horses out early in the morning for a ride at the beach or in the mountains, I cleaned up my horse the night before and kept him in that night. I might even put a stable sheet on him—not a heavy blanket, just a light sheet. He would look nice and I wouldn't have to spend time cleaning him in the morning.

The next morning I'd get up early, run down, throw him his feed then go back and shower and dress and eat my breakfast. He would have his breakfast eaten and be ready to go. All I had to do was load him into my truck and take off. Those little things meant a lot. I liked a clean, good looking horse I could be proud of. I wanted him to look the best he could.

If I let him run at night then caught him that morning, he was wet if it had been wet at all during the night. He didn't dry off and it was hard to have a clean animal.

My loafing shed off the barn had three sides. To keep him in,

I would put up a two-by-ten board across the open end of the loafing shed so I had him trapped in where it was dry. He couldn't get out, of course, to urinate or defecate. He would come into the barn to do that because he spent most of his time in the loafing shed and wanted to keep it clean. I got to thinking about that and decided I was going to do something to make him want to go outside the stall in the loafing shed to relieve himself.

I went to the far end of the loafing shed and dug a four-foot-by-four-foot-by-four-foot pit. I filled three feet of the pit with big river rock, an inch and a half or bigger so it would drain well. Then I dumped a bale of shavings over the rocks. It worked from the minute I fixed that horse latrine. That's exactly where he would urinate and defecate.

As you travel in the West, you find different kinds of rigging. Rigging, is the cowboy term for tack. Down in Texas and in the deep Southwest almost every saddle you see has a full double-rigging, which is a saddle with a front cinch and a flank cinch. Draw a line straight down from the saddle horn and that is where the D-ring hangs and where the front cinch falls.

In Northern Nevada, Eastern Oregon and Idaho, you see a lot of seven-eighths and three-quarter double-rigged saddles. On a seven-eighths double rigging, the front cinch comes down about one inch to the rear of the saddle horn. A three-quarter double rigging has the front cinch about two inches behind the straight line down from the saddle horn. Many of the old saddle makers in that part of the country don't make anything else. I have seen a lot of saddles from Sandy in Burns, Oregon, and a seven-eighths or three-quarter rigged saddle is the only kind he would build.

In Oregon where we have many mountains and the horse is going up and down hill, he is better off with seven-eighths double rigging. A horse going down hill with a full double rigging has the cinch riding up front and it will wear a sore behind his front legs. The seven-eighths double-rigged saddle gets the cinch back just enough so it's not up under the horse's front elbow.

It's easier for me to keep a saddle up on a horse's withers where it belongs with a seven-eighths or three-quarter double rigging. A full double rigging tends to slide back too far.

The flank cinch remains at the same place on all the riggings. The flank cinch is there for a purpose, as everything in cowboy wear is. It's for roping big animals—steers and cows.

In my opinion, with a seven-eighths or three-quarter double-rigged saddle, you do not need a flank cinch if you are doing light roping such as small, young calves. The front cinch is back to where it's holding both ends of the saddle down.

In competitive roping, all ropers use a flank cinch and have it snugged up, not tight but snug, on the horse's belly. When a roper has his rope tied hard and fast to the saddle horn, then drops the rope around that calf's neck, does a fast stop and throws the calf, the flank cinch keeps the saddle from coming up and pinching the horse's withers. Hurting a horse's withers spoils a good roping horse real quick. He won't want to stop fast and is soon ducking that rope.

Often, I see a pleasure or trail rider's flank cinch hanging one to eight inches below the horse's belly. This can cause big problems.

A horse kicking at a fly can get his foot hung in that flank cinch and then there is hell to pay. In riding through a downfall of tree limbs, the horse can step on one end of a long branch and cause the other end to poke up so the branch goes up under that flank cinch. Whoever is riding that horse is going to have a big surprise. It's a real chance to get hurt.

A flank cinch should always be kept snug on the horse's belly. Unless you are doing some serious roping you do not need a flank cinch. It is unnecessary baggage. My flank cinch hangs in my tack room when I am not roping.

The US Cavalry knew a lot about horses and they did a lot of things right. The old Army saddle, the McClellan, was a center-fire rigged saddle. The cinch came right down the middle of the saddle. There wasn't a place for two cinches. However, the cinch could be adjusted a little more forward or a little back. Most people rode that McClellan saddle with that cinch straight down.

The foundation of a saddle is a wooden tree made out of pine, covered with wet untanned beef hide. The hide has been scraped free of hair and soaked in water. The hide is laced up tight on the saddle tree, and when it shrinks onto that pine, it makes the tree almost as strong as iron.

There are three or four different kinds of saddle trees to fit the horse. The trouble is that you don't buy a saddle for one horse. I have owned many horses and my saddle had to make do for the horse I had at the time.

A standard tree fits a horse with good withers. When I say good withers, I mean sharp, pointed withers. Many of the Quarter horses today have developed wide withers, known as mutton withers. Sharp withers make a healthier, longer lasting, more sound horse than mutton withers.

You might think, well, I have a Quarter horse, maybe I should get a Quarter horse tree. But if you get that saddle and put it on a Thoroughbred or a horse with good withers, the bottom of the swell of the saddle rides right on top of his withers. This pinches the withers and causes problems.

I would not buy a Quarter horse tree unless I had a horse I thought the world of and had to fit him specifically. Otherwise, I would buy a standard tree. Most standard trees fit most Quarter horses.

The swell is that part on either side of the saddle horn. A pure roping saddle has no swell. It has, of course, a horn and some horns stick up pretty high because they are used all the time to dally on. A roping saddle is made to be easy and quick to get out of. You have seen the cowboys in a rodeo. When they catch that steer and pull the horse to a stop, they are on the ground before the horse's front feet come down from the stop. Their saddles probably have no swell and their cantles are only an inch or an inch and a half high.

A cutting saddle or bucking saddle has a large swell. Some of those swells are shaped so they extend out from the saddle so a rider can get his upper legs under the swell and stay on the saddle. The cantleboard is deep, maybe four or five inches. The cantleboard or cantle is the part that rises on the back of the seat. Some of the old saddles had eight-inch cantles. They came halfway up the rider's back.

The cutting or bucking saddle is going to fit the rider as near as it can. Where the horse is moving fast and making fast turns cutting cattle, the rider has to stay right with the horse. A saddle that has big swells on the front and a deep cantle on the back helps a guy stay in the saddle a whole lot longer if a horse bucks or shies quickly.

I try my best not to get on a bucking horse or one that is going to buck or one that has anything like that in his mind. Therefore, I have always ridden a roping saddle. For me, it is much more comfortable than a deeper saddle.

Saddles come in different sizes from a twelve-inch seat to a seventeen-inch seat. Trees are measured from the saddle horn back to the front part of the cantle. A fourteen- to fifteen-one-half-inch tree fits most everyone. A sixteen- or seventeen-inch tree on a saddle puts the weight farther back on the horse and makes it harder for the horse to carry the rider.

A horse is made to carry the weight on his front feet. His back feet propel him; his front feet carry the load. So you want to keep your weight as much over the withers as you can. I'm a big guy and I ride a fifteen-inch saddle tree. I am very comfortable in it.

If I were getting a new saddle today, I would try to have one made even though it would be expensive. A good saddle today runs from fifteen hundred up to three thousand dollars. I would buy one with seven-eighths rigging. And I would hang the flank cinch in my tack room.

I have used all different kinds of saddle pads. I was never satisfied with a saddle pad until the last fifteen years or so. It is almost impossible to go on long rides in hot weather without scalding a horse's back. Almost every saddle horse you see, if he has covered a lot of ground or had any experience, has white marks on each side of his withers. Those marks are caused by scalds. That's where the most pressure is from the saddle on the horse.

The scalds come from hot weather and pads that don't give the back a chance to breathe. The old felt pads, in my opinion, are not good for a horse. They look thick and feel fairly soft, but they smother a horse's back and scald it.

The best saddle pad is a Coolback pad. These pads are made out of material used beneath hospital patients to prevent bedsores. They look like sheepskin but they are man-made fabric. They are about two inches thick including the air in them. They come in different colors. I liked the white ones because I could tell when they were dirty. I always carried two or three Coolback Pads. I changed them when I was riding hard. I washed them when they got dirty.

Laundromats don't like to have saddle blankets washed in their machines because of the hair. I had an old-fashioned wringer washing machine I used to wash my saddle blankets. I filled it with cold water and then put the saddle blankets in and let them agitate. I kept changing the water until it was clean.

The old Navajo blankets that were one hundred percent wool were good. Any one hundred percent wool pad is better on a horse's back than anything else other than the cool pad. I still have three of those old time Navajo blankets. I usually put one of the Navajos over my Coolback pad. The many-colored Navajo blanket dressed the horse up as well as providing more padding.

I used a tackaberry cinch with sheepskin padding behind it. The sheepskin lies next to the horse. The latigo loops through the top part of the tackaberry so the tackaberry is always on the saddle. When you saddle the horse, you simply pull the cinch ring up and hang it on the tackaberry to lock it, then tighten the latigo and tie it. It was quick, and my horse never had any cinch galls with the tackaberry. Cinch galls normally occur right where the latigo loops into the cinch ring or right behind the horse's elbow in front.

For pleasure riding I used big bell-type or pear-shaped roping stirrups. The three-inch wide tread was comfortable when I spent all day in the saddle. The narrow tread on the narrow oxbow type stirrups used for bucking horses made my feet sore on long days.

I also used working-type tapaderos, known as taps, over the stirrups. Here in the Northwest I could be in rain or snow in the mountains most any time. When my feet were hitting wet brush, it was just like turning a hose on them. It forced water through my boots and my feet were wet in five minutes. With taps, it didn't matter how cold it was or if there was snow or water on the brush. My feet stayed dry. I almost hated to get off my horse when it was snowing or raining because my feet were dry in my stirrups covered by my taps.

Tapaderos cost fifty or seventy-five dollars to have made, but they are worth their weight in gold for an outdoor rider. When I had Garth Bonney in The Dalles make my last saddle thirty years or so ago, I had him make a pair of taps to put over my roping stirrups. I was never without them when I was riding outside.

I used a split-ear headstall and a silver-mounted bit. On either side of the headstall, just below the ear, was a sterling silver piece. Down each side of the headstall were sterling silver figurines: a spade, a heart, a club and a diamond. You don't have to have silver on a bridle, of course. Well-kept leather looks good, that's for sure.

I have a headstall in my tack room right now that was made by an old rawhider here in Oregon—Lee Nichols. Lee was one of the best rawhide braiders in the country.

If a horse had a good head, I always liked to show off his head without a browband or throatlatch, so I usually rode a split-ear headstall. But you can get into trouble with one. One time in the mountains we were stopped at a watering trough. My horse had had his drink. While the other riders and I were standing there talking, my horse scratched himself against a tree. I'll be dadgummed if he didn't rub that bridle off and leave it hanging right there in that tree. Here I was sitting on my horse without a bridle or bit in his mouth. Luckily other horses were there and he stayed still. I got off and put it back on him.

I used a plain curb grazing bit with a chin strap or curb strap. These bits are easy on a horse. All your leverage on a curb bit comes from the chin strap. You shouldn't use a chain under his chin unless you know what you are doing. If you're not thinking, you can pull harder than you should and that chain can get rough. If a horse has been trained properly, he doesn't need a chain. A soft curb strap does the job.

Of course, on a colt or a young horse that is still in training and not used to a bit in his mouth, a snaffle bit is best.

Many people ride older trained horses with a hackamore. A hackamore has nothing in the horse's mouth. Control on a hackamore is through the braided rawhide piece over the horse's nose. This can be placed just right so it gives good control over an animal.

Many hackamores come with a mecate rope on them. The rope fastens to one side of the hackamore, comes over the horse's neck for the rider to use as a rein, and fastens to the other side of the hackamore. A second rope fastens to the bottom of the hackamore at the horse's chin. This rope is eight to ten feet long. The rider tucks the end of the rope under his belt. If he gets unloaded, he'll have that rope in his hand when he hits the ground so the horse won't get away from him.

I have used all types of reins. The advantage of split reins is that you can use them to tap your horse to keep him going, use them in place of a quirt or bat. Otherwise, there is no need to have split reins. I am not talking about training now, I am talking about a finished horse you are pleasure riding. Lee Nichols made me a nice pair of split reins that are long and usable. Split reins should be at least eight feet long; you need at least three feet hanging over to tap your horse.

Most of the time I used a roping rein. This is one rein that's about six feet long. It fastens to the right side of the bit, comes over the horse's neck and fastens to the left side of the bit. You hold it in the middle. The one rein was much handier when I was roping where I had to manage the rein with my left hand which also held the slack rope of the lariat. If I had had split reins sticking out with a rope swinging around, I would have been in trouble.

Many people use braided rawhide reins in this country. I tried them once, but they were hard on my hands. If I wasn't wearing gloves and the horse jerked on the reins, they acted just like a file. They would almost take the skin off my hands.

I always used a braided rawhide bosal. Lee Nichols made mine. A bosal is a nose piece that goes around the horse's nose just above his mouth. A leather head piece goes behind the horse's ears and down each side to hold the nose piece on the animal. I put the bosal on first, then put the bridle over that.

I always had a mecate rope along. I used a half-inch fiberglass soft rope about ten feet long. I kept it in a coil about six inches in diameter. I kept that under my lariat where it hung right in the middle of the lariat when they were both hanging on the saddle.

When we stopped for lunch or to doctor a calf or do other ground work, I tied my horse. I put the mecate rope around his neck and tied a bowline knot, ran the rope end through the ring at the bottom of the bosal, and then tied it to a tree or something stout.

I could also bring the mecate end back to me on the saddle. I tucked it under my belt where it could come loose if it had to, or tied it to the saddle. If I tied it to the saddle, I tied it in a slip knot on a saddle string to the left side of my saddle tree.

The main reason for the bosal and mecate was to tie my horse without tying him by his bridle. Tying a horse with the bridle reins is asking for trouble. Sooner or later you are going to have broken reins or a broken bridle. Another horse will take a bite at him or something will spook him and he will jump back. If the bridle breaks and drags that bit out through his teeth, it could chip a tooth or two.

I saw a bridle break when I was helping gather cattle a few miles above the Robertson ranch at Drewsey, Oregon. We had gone into what they called the "burn," and had gathered several hundred head of mother cows, all with calves, and some bulls. We were going up to the Forest Service reserve line from west to northeast.

There is a real bad spot they call the jungle. It was hard to drive cows through there. They would turn back, scatter and get into the brush, lodgepole pine thickets and mahogany thickets. The Robertsons had built an extra fence. This made a fenceline on either side—the Forest Service boundary fence on one side and the newer fence on the other side. This let us poke the cattle down from the top. Two or three riders would get at the bottom and push the cattle on another mile or two to the Forest Reserve line. We were coming down that chute with the tail end of the bunch. We had three or four riders and the others were down below.

A calf had wedged itself into the crotch of a tree so Rod Robertson and another cowboy had to go down and get it. Rod jumped off his horse and handed the reins to Rose Robertson. She also held the other guy's horse.

The calf got under the fence. Rod and the other guy got on the other side of the fence and chased him down, then walked on down the rest of the way.

Rod had a brand new headstall. It was silver mounted and he was proud of it. Rod usually rode with a roping rein with a romal on the end that he could use to bat cattle along. So Rose threw Rod's roping rein over the saddle horn of the other empty horse that she was leading. This was rough country. It is straight down and all timber and brush.

I said, "Hey, Rose, I'll get that horse."

She didn't hear me. I was trying to get down to them and she was moving. Then Rod's horse stumbled and there went the headstall. One cheek of the bridle broke and the bit pulled out of the horse's mouth. Rod was really disappointed. Here the horse comes with his new headstall all busted.

When I left, I took that headstall home with me to have it repaired in Portland. That might sound funny. Here I come out of ranch country where everybody's working with horses and cattle and have the headstall fixed in metropolitan Portland. But there are more saddle shops and more leathersmiths in the metropolitan area because there are more horses. There are many more saddle horses around the cities than there are in the ranch country simply because there are more people.

In the mountainous country of the Northwest, a breast collar is indispensable. It keeps the saddle from sliding back when the horse is climbing steep hills. I attached mine to the cinch ring on either side of the saddle.

A breast collar should be what its name implies—a breast collar—and be adjusted properly. One that comes up too high on the horse's throat tends to cut off his wind.

Lining the breast collar with sheepskin helps minimize rubbing. Even with sheepskin, if you are working hard, riding all day long with a lot of uphill and downhill, a breast collar will wear a spot on each side of the front shoulder of the horse.

I put the sheepskin lining on my breast collar myself. Any saddle shop carries sheepskin. I made a pattern on the sheepskin using the breast collar and cut it out. I cemented the sheepskin on the collar with the fleece towards the horse. I used leather cement and followed the instructions for applying it. It's better if the lining isn't sewn, so it can be pulled off and replaced when it gets worn.

A saddle that fits properly and a guy who is riding correctly keeps the weight up over a horse's withers. Just think about a jockey in a horse race or steeplechase. Even though he might weigh only one hundred ten pounds, that jockey holds his weight right square over his horse's withers, not over the back end. The farther back he goes, even with that light weight, the more handicap he's putting on his horse.

Keep that in mind when you load gear on a horse. Anything you put behind your saddle in saddlebags is where a horse doesn't do the best job of handling weight. Saddlebags rest on a horse where he is most vulnerable to weight—over his kidneys.

I have often seen saddlebags misused. I've seen them tied on the horse so they flopped around or rode back too far. I have seen saddlebags that hold thirty pounds of gear.

I owned two pair of saddlebags. I had an old Army pair that were pear-shaped. They were small at the top to keep things from jiggling out and larger at the bottom. They were made for the US Cavalry for them to carry their extra socks or pair of longjohns or whatever in that saddlebag.

I used another pair for day rides, which I used ninety-eight percent of the time. Garth Bonney in The Dalles, who made my saddle, made these saddlebags. They were just nine inches square. The gusset was two and one half inches, so they were only two and one half inches thick. The flap was made out of good latigo leather and had one strap, rather than two or three straps. I found that one strap made it much easier to get into my saddlebag when I was on my horse. If I wanted to reach in and get a candy bar or a compass, I only had to undo one strap.

My saddlebags fit up under the cantle on the back of the saddle, snugged up to the little saddle strings on each side of the saddle. Those strings were about five inches long. There were two holes in the leather on each side of the saddlebags where those two strings went through. The two holes were about three-eighths inch apart. I put the two strings through and tied a single regular knot. That held the saddlebag snug against the cantle and held it there all day long. The saddle bag itself came close to my thigh, which meant I had most of the weight as far forward as possible.

It had plenty of room for packing my lunch, my rain hat cover and a get-lost kit. My kit included a canister of waterproof matches, fire starter, rattlesnake bite kit and that type of thing. There was room for a small thermos bottle, although I never carried a thermos. I carried a tin cup so if I ran into a good spring I could get a drink of water. I always had trouble drinking water if I was lying down.

I learned to ride years ago with spurs, and I think it's the proper route to go. I have heard a lot of people say, "Oh, I wouldn't use spurs because it's cruel." That is not true. Spurs, when used properly, are simply a reminder to the horse that you are the boss.

I wore a pair of fairly long-shanked spurs. When I wanted something from the horse, all I had to do was touch him with the spurs and he came to immediate attention. I don't think I ever in my life drew blood from a horse using spurs. Anyone who uses spurs properly does not have to hurt the horse. Those spurs on your heels simply give you that much more control over that big one-thousand- to thirteen-hundred-pound animal that you are sitting on.

Spurs should be used in the cinch area, either on the shoulder or right behind the cinch, but not any further back. Even a gentle horse will buck if it feels spurs in the flank area.

I would not get on a strange horse with spurs, however. An older horse that is not used to spurs would probably buck the minute he was touched with spurs. But you can teach even an older horse to accept spurs.

I remember when Debbie Robertson got a new pair of spurs. She was riding Elmer Fudd, one of her favorite horses. Elmer was four years old, and Debbie had been using him about a year.

She went out one morning with her brand new spurs on. Everyone was getting ready to ride. She got up on Elmer and went to pull him around and touched him with the offside spur. Elmer threw Debbie up in the air. Debbie hung up those spurs for a long time. Eventually she put them back on and got Elmer used to them.

A good way to get a horse used to spurs is to work with him on the ground. Take the spur in your hand and push on his side right where your heels would hit him. Work both sides of the horse with that spur. Then after you have come back from a long ride and the horse is tired, put the spurs on and ride around with them for a bit. Touch him lightly with them. From the ground work, you will have gotten him to where he's not jumping out of his skin when you touch him with the spurs.

You soon learn that it's second nature to not drive those spurs in. You just touch him with those spurs and he responds much quicker than he ever did to a bat or your heel.

I have watched many people ride horses without spurs, They were constantly kicking the horses with their heels, and kicking hard. Sometimes they would spread their legs out as far as they could, then come back and thump their horses with their heels. The horses didn't pay any attention to them. With spurs you lightly touch the horse. It isn't even noticeable to a spectator. You have a much better horseback ride if you ride with spurs.

I have a beautiful old rawhide lariat. It's seventy feet long with no joints in it. These lariats are hard to find and I would not take a couple hundred dollars for it. I'd love to use it for roping, but I'm afraid I might get in an accident and break it.

It has been taken care of properly so it's fairly soft. I have a recipe from an old rawhider for dressing that really takes care of rawhide. Here it is.

Take two or three pounds of beef tallow and render it into oil. Do the same thing with an equal amount of beeswax. Mix the beeswax and the rendered-out beef tallow together, fifty-fifty, and let it cool a little bit. Pour this into cupcake papers. Let it sit out to cool and harden.

Rub those cakes into the rawhide to keep it supple and strong.

When traveling with my horse, I took along a tray or box similar to a horseshoer's tray. It had an extra set of everything in it, so it was always ready to go. I had brushes, curry combs and medicine. I had a little slot in it where I kept a rectal thermometer for my horse.

I always took along first aid medicine and bandaging. I learned to do that the hard way, by running into problems when I was up in the hills and not having anything to work with. For instance, if a horse gashes his leg on old barb wire or whatever, you're better off if you can put some lightly medicated salve on it until you can get to a doctor and get it sewn up. A bandage for animals that sticks to itself is really handy. I had that in my first aid tray.

Dr. Brent Milleson, who is a veterinarian, has taken care of my horses ever since he got out of college. He fixed up a mixture of DMSO and Furasin ointment to use on a gash or cut that doesn't need to be sewed up. I also used the mixture after a horse had been sewn up, to dress the wound with and I kept the scab pulled off so it didn't make a big scab or deep scar.

I don't think I was ever up in the mountains that I didn't use some of my first aid kit. If I didn't need it for my horse, someone in the crowd needed it for his.

A good fly spray to wipe on a horse is important in the mountains. Horse flies and other insects can drive a horse crazy, especially if he is tied up. I always had some Wipe, which is a Farnam product. This is most effective if you rub it in against the grain of the horse's hair. It lasts longer than the spray-on type. The spray goes on easier and it's not as messy, but you have to use more of it and use it more often.

I also made my own fly spray, which worked very well and was cheaper. I mixed one-half water and one-half rubbing alcohol and added about one or two ounces of Oil of Citronella. I sprayed that on my horse, then took an old towel and rubbed it in against the grain.

I also made a spray that I used for grooming the horse's mane and tail. I used the same formula as above but added about ten percent mineral oil. I shook it up, of course, to mix the alcohol, water and oil then sprayed it on the tail. It made the tail easy to comb and, with the Citronella, made a good stay-away fan for flies.

A saddle will last almost forever if you take care of it. Leather needs to be clean. When dirt gets into leather, it starts drying it out, making the leather brittle and wearing it out. Most of the saddles I see today are dry and need attention.

It's important to take a saddle apart at least once a year and scrub everything. I did mine twice a year. The horse sweats on the saddle and it dries out.

I took a lesson on taking care of saddles from one of the old time German saddlemakers from one of the old saddle shops in Portland, Oregon. I am talking about the early days. They closed around 1950. Heide and Streibe was the name. Their saddlemakers were from the old country and they made excellent saddles. I think the saddlemaker's name was Heine. He told me the best way to take care of a saddle was with saddle soap.

I didn't know anything at the time. The only thing I had done with saddle soap was to use the stuff in a can and put it on like shoe polish and rub it in.

Heine said, "Lord, no, that's not the way to use saddle soap. Saddle soap is a soap. You need to wash your saddle with it. Get a good bar of glycerin-based saddle soap. Dampen a sponge with warm water if you can get it, cold if you can't. With that sponge work up a tough lather," he said. "Scrub that saddle like you were washing walls. Wash it good. Let the soap dry on the saddle, then wipe it off with a clean towel."

"Take the saddle apart. Take the stirrups off. Take the flank cinch off. Take all the leather off: the offside billet, the latigo, everything. Take all the conchos off. Take the knots out of the saddle strings," he said.

So I have always done what he told me. I take everything off I can get off. I even take the conchos off the tapaderos. But, I don't take all the knots out of the saddle strings at once because those knots are complicated. I leave some so I can see how to put the others back together.

I have a hook high up on the wall where I hang the leather pieces. That way I can hold the other end of a leather piece and saddle soap it real good, instead of trying to clean it on a bench or table.

I have an old aluminum ice tray to hold the saddle soap. It fits just right. I saddle soap that saddle from one end to the other. I let the soap dry, then wipe it off with a clean towel. You can't use too much saddle soap, The more you use, the better it is. That glycerin soaks into the leather and makes it soft and pliable.

I also use Lexol, which is a leather dressing, instead of oil, a tip I got from Heine. I coat the smooth side of the leather on the whole saddle with Lexol while it is still apart. I use eight or ten coats rather than slopping it on.

When it's clean, the saddle looks completely different than when I took it apart, especially if it had that old light-colored look, was starting to curl up and become stiff and dry. Sometimes if a saddle has gone a long time between cleanings, it takes two or three applications like this to get the saddle looking right.

When I finish the saddle soaping and the Lexol, I put the saddle back together. Then I take a bottle of Feibing's Tan-Kote and cover it. Tan-Kote is a sealer to help keep the oils in the saddle. It really shines it.

I keep a big sponge just for this. I get the sponge wet and wring the excess water out of it. Then I shake the Tan-Kote real well and pour the Tan-Kote on the sponge. I squeeze the sponge to get the Tan-Kote in the sponge. Then I put it on my saddle as if I am painting it. I cover the whole saddle and my saddlebags with Tan-Kote, but not to excess, then let it dry.

I have the prettiest saddle you ever saw. It looks twice as good as a new saddle because it's been used. The saddle soap and Lexol bring the color back, but it's darker; it has that cherry red mahogany color that looks like a million dollars.

I never oil my saddle seat or most of the other parts. If the skirts are getting a little stiff, I might use a little oil on them. The one place I do use oil and I use plenty of it is on the stirrup leathers. I don't mean the fenders, just the stirrup leathers, the part that goes up under the saddle, the part that actually supports my weight. I take the stirrups off. Then, I pull the stirrup leathers out on one side, but not all the way out because they are hard to get back. Usually they are stiff and dry.

I warm up a bit of Neatsfoot oil and put the Neatsfoot on a piece of sheepskin and use that to apply the oil to the leathers. I put a lot of Neatsfoot oil on those stirrup leathers. Otherwise they wear out within a few years. If they are really dry, I oil the leathers on both sides. If they are not real dry, I oil them on the smooth side only. If I keep them oiled and pliable, they will last forever. I am not going to wind up standing up in my stirrups one day and have the stirrup break and off I go.

I don't oil any other part of the saddle. It's too hard to get out. If I got too much oil on it, the leather would stay sticky, oily and greasy.

Of course, I clean all my leather equipment—headstalls, bridle reins, and so on. On my silver-inlaid headstall I have fourteen pieces of silver to take off. They all come off except for two pieces just below each ear, which can't come off. I unbuckle everything and straighten it out. I take the bit and reins off.

Where the leather holds the bit, it is usually dry and chapped. I can hardly straighten it out it's so stiff. I saddle soap the inside of that just like I do the outside until it's soft and pliable. I clean the bridle reins until they are soft and pliable. Then I use Lexol and Tan-Kote on the leather. I polish the silver with silver polish.

I use the same treatment on my chaps. Chaps or leggings get very dry and stiff over the years. I have seen some I could lean up against the wall and they wouldn't cave in. Wearing a soft, pliable pair of leather chaps beats the heck out of a pair that are half stiff. Not only are they easier to wear, they shed water much better.

People who ranch usually don't have time to care for their saddles like this. When I go to the Robertson Ranch in the spring, we spend three days cleaning their saddles and gear. They didn't do this before I started going up there. They liked the look of my gear so much that they wanted me to help them get started. So every year we have a saddle cleaning session. It really makes a difference in those saddles.

13   *The eternal nine-year-old horse*

I am over eighty years old now and I have learned that when you're horse trading, it's real easy to get stung. One of the common hazards is buying an old horse if it doesn't have papers to prove its age.

It's fairly easy for an experienced horseman to tell a horse's age up to about nine years by the condition of the teeth. After that, a horse is smooth-mouthed and it's much harder to figure age. I have seen many horses seventeen and over that have been sold as nine year olds.

I can pretty well tell a horse's age, but a long time ago I took a hint from Red Harper. Red didn't want to hurt people's feelings unless they made him mad.

People would come in and say, "Red, look at my horse. Tell me how old he is."

Red would look at the horse. While he was looking, he'd say, "Well, how old is he supposed to be?"

The answer would be, "They told me he was around nine."

Red would look the horse over, walk around him and say, "Well, I think that's about right."

He would never look at a horse's mouth and say, "This horse is fourteen." He knew that the person did not want to know his horse was older than nine.

So I do the same thing when somebody asks me to look at their horse's mouth and tell them how old it is. A few years back a little gal lived close to us and bought a pony—nine years old, of course.

My good friend and neighbor next door, Bob Eastman, looked at the horse's mouth and said, "Yeah, that's about right."

I looked at the mouth and the horse was probably fifteen or sixteen. I looked at Bob; Bob looked at me.

I said, "Yeah, I think that's close."

Why hurt her feelings? She loved the horse and it would never make any difference to her how old it was.

Telling the age of a horse was a great mystery to me for a long time. Red Harper, an old horse trader from The Dalles, was the first person I knew who could tell the age of a horse by looking into his mouth. He could tell a horse's age up to thirty years old.

I would say, "Hey, Red, tell me how you can tell the age of a horse by his teeth."

Red would go into a long explanation and I wouldn't know any more when he got through than when he started. For a long time I thought that these old timers just didn't like to give up that kind of information. It finally dawned on me that Red could not explain what he was looking for.

I have had a chart on my tack room wall for a long time. The whole chart is about horse's teeth and how to tell the age of a horse by looking at his teeth. The chart has about fifty illustrations and an explanation for each illustration.

I ordered the chart from an ad in the *Western Horseman*. It came from Forest Farms Western Store, 168 N. Fulton Avenue, Rochester, Indiana 46975. These charts are available, if not from this place, from others. Somebody at the *Western Horseman* magazine would know where you could pick one up.

When I first got it, the chart looked so complicated that I really didn't study it much for years. As it unfolds, telling a horse's age by his teeth is not that complicated. You can look at the chart and in a horse's mouth and easily tell a horse's age up until the age of nine. After that, it's a bit more difficult.

A colt's baby teeth come in quickly after he's foaled. He keeps these teeth until he is about two and one half years old. Then he starts shedding them and getting his permanent set of incisors in front. This process goes on until he is about four and one half years old.

He has twelve incisors, six upper and six lower. The two teeth that are right in the center of the mouth in the lower jaw and upper jaw are called nippers. They do most of the work and they start wearing.

The two teeth on either side of those are called the center teeth because they are between the nippers and the corner teeth. The other two incisors are called the corner teeth. Those are around on the side of the horse's mouth.

Two hook teeth, one on each side, sit just back of the corner incisors with a small space between.

The teeth in the back of the mouth are molars or "grinding teeth." There is a large space between the molars and the two hook teeth. This is where the horse's bit fits.

Some horses have so-called wolf teeth just in front of the molars in the upper jaw. They are hard to see and they don't happen in every horse. Wolf teeth can cause a horse a lot of trouble. They are easily extracted by a veterinarian.

A horse's teeth should be examined yearly by a veterinarian. After ten years, they should be checked every six months and floated, if necessary.

Sometimes, especially in older horses, the molars wear unevenly. Some may protrude farther than others, which keeps the molars from meeting. When this happens, the grinding effect is lost and feed passes through without the horse getting the value out of it. A veterinarian can level those teeth with a tool similar to a large file.

As the teeth all wear, the age of the horse becomes apparent.

At the age of five years old, the incisors are wide from side to side and narrow from front to back.

On a twelve-year-old horse, the nippers are almost round. The center teeth are not quite as round, but almost. They might still show a little bit of the flat part towards the side. The corner teeth are still rather flat. They are just starting to get round on the edge toward the center of the mouth.

The teeth haven't changed shape; they have simply worn down.

At the age of twenty, all those lower six teeth in front have gone from round to pretty much triangular.

From twenty to thirty years old, the teeth simply start getting wider from front to back and narrower from side to side so that the teeth at thirty years old are very triangular. The teeth are at least twice as thick as they are wide.

It isn't that complicated and it is nice to be able to look into a horse's mouth and come pretty close to his age. There are many cold-blooded horses—horses without papers—that are over twenty years old and sell for ten years old because most people cannot tell their age.

This happens even with honest people. Let's say they bought the horse when he was about sixteen years old but the person they bought him from told them, "Well, he's about nine years old."

So they keep him five years and sell him. The buyer wants to know how old he is. They say, "Well, let's see, we've had him only a few years, he must be about thirteen years old." So now the horse is selling for not over fourteen years old if he lives to be thirty-five.

A couple years ago I was up in the mountains rounding up cattle in August. We were gathering them, holding them and then driving them down out of the mountains to the next Forest Service allotment where they would remain until they came out in October. A friend of mine, Bob Christensen, was there. He lives in Burns and has a small ranch of his own and also runs a business. He was riding a big strong Thoroughbred-type sorrel gelding. The horse obviously had a little age on him.

Bob said, "Someone told me you could age a horse."

I told him I could come pretty close.

I looked in the horse's mouth, at both his lower jaw and upper jaw. The middle teeth in the lower jaw were all very wide from front to back and very narrow from side to side. The teeth in the upper jaw were pretty well triangular yet. The upper jaw doesn't mature as fast as the lower jaw, but it confirms what you're looking at in the lower jaw. I said, "Bob, do you really want to know how old he is?"

He said, "Yeah, I think I know."

I said, "Let me tell you what I think. He's got to be about twenty-five years old."

Bob smiled. He said, "I've known that horse for a long time and the guy who sold him to me told me how old he was. According to what he told me, the horse would be twenty years old now. But," he said, "another friend of mine who knew both of us told me that the horse was five years older than that."

So I had hit it on the button.

Bob said, "You know, I really like to ride him; he's been a good horse. But I'm going to retire this horse from heavy work. I'm just going to keep him around the pasture, ride him a little bit in there. He's getting too old for this hard work up here in the mountains."

The next year he didn't have the big old Thoroughbred sorrel with him.

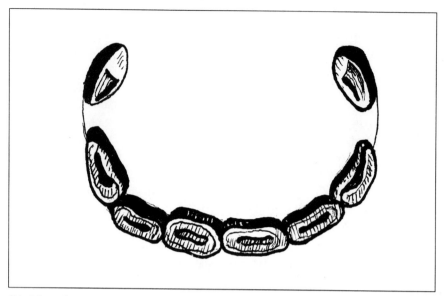

Looking down at the bottom incisors and hook teeth of a six-year-old horse. The cups, that is, the indented area of the teeth, are easy to see (shown as dark areas in the drawing). The incisors are wide from side to side and narrow from from to back. (Illustration byWoody Cooper)

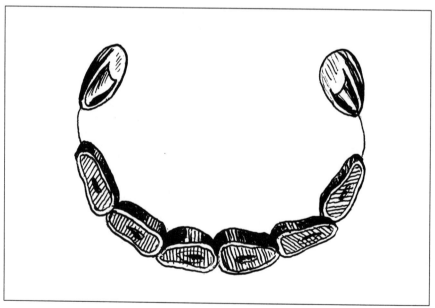

Looking down at the bottom teeth of an eight-year-old horse. The cups have begun to wear away, but the teeth are still fairly wide from side to side. (Illustration by Woody Cooper)

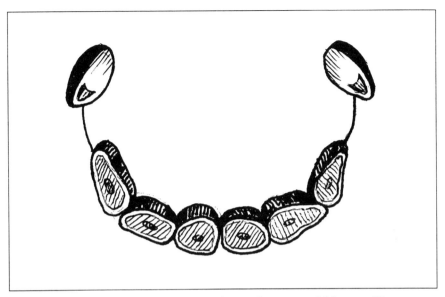

Looking down at the bottom teeth of a twelve-year-old horse. The cups are very shallow, and the teeth are losing their elongate form from side to side and look fairly round. (Illustration by Woody Cooper)

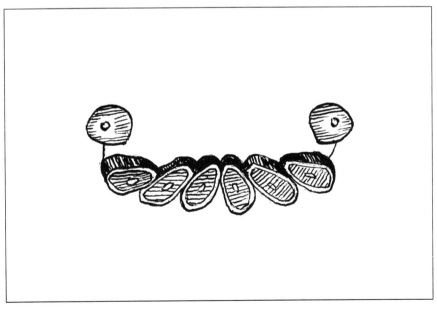

Looking down at the bottom teeth of a twenty-six-year-old horse. The cups are almost gone, the teeth are narrower from side to side than from front to back. (Illustraton by Woody Cooper)

It was June of 1972 and I was fifty-seven years old. All my life I had fooled with horses. I had wanted to experience a cowboy's life and now here I was, helping move 250 pairs of cattle into Oregon's Strawberry mountains. My being here was pure chance, beginning with events I had absolutely no part in.

Guy Marshall was the attorney for Mayflower Farms, the company I worked for. Over the years Guy and I had become good friends.

Guy came out of law school and went into the firm of Clark and Clark in Portland, Oregon. It was an old, steady, conservative law firm. Guy bought the business in the mid-1950s when the last partner, Malcolm Clark, retired. In the file he found a deed to a half-section of land in Eastern Oregon. He asked Malcolm about it and Malcolm told Guy he had taken the property in on a trade years ago. He had never seen it.

Guy purchased that land from Malcolm. Then he went to Eastern Oregon to see what it looked like. The description of it took him forty-five miles east of Burns to the little town of Drewsey, Oregon, an old ranching community. At that time about sixteen people lived in the town. There was a general store, a post office, a garage and a few houses. It served all the ranchers along the Middle Fork of the Malheur River, around Drewsey, and the ranchers in Otis Valley about six miles north of Drewsey.

Guy drove to Otis Valley and knocked at the door of Bill Robertson, who agreed to help him find his land. Guy and Bill, along with Glenn Sitz, another rancher in the area, drove around the country. They finally located Guy's half-section of land. The land had a good spring on it and sat in the middle of a BLM allotment on which Bill Robertson was running his cattle.

Guy and his wife, Lou, built a cabin on the land. Guy used the cabin as a base for hunting deer and elk. I always kidded Guy that he was the only person I knew who had a cabin so remote that he had to have a map to get to it every time he went there.

Over the years, Guy and Lou became good friends with Glenn Sitz and Bill Robertson. Glenn ran a good-sized cattle operation. He did that with one hired man and help from his family and neighbors.

Guy told Glenn that he had a friend down in the Willamette Valley who had his own horse. Of course, that friend was me.

Guy said, "He's crazy about the outdoors. He'd love to come up here and ride with you when you're moving cattle."

Glenn said, "Fine, we can always use the help anytime he wants to come. We're going to drive the cattle up to the mountains on June first. We'll be gathering them here and cutting out the pairs to go up there. Your friend can come and stay in the house."

Guy told Glenn that I would bring my own horse and my trailer to stay in. I didn't realize it then, but Glenn was tickled to death to have some help moving those cattle up into the mountains. It's a big job and another rider and another horse, even though inexperienced, help.

Otis Valley is three hundred and fifty miles from Wilsonville. Guy gave me all the particulars on how to get there. He said he had me fixed up with Glenn Sitz. I hadn't met Glenn nor anyone in Otis Valley.

I took a week's vacation. My wife, Grace, went with me. I loaded up my horse into the horse van on my pickup. I pulled a twenty-one-foot Terry vacation trailer behind it.

We headed over the Cascade Mountains down into Bend and across the High Desert to Burns. Forty-five miles on the east side of Burns we turned off at a sign that pointed to Drewsey, just two miles north.

We drove into Drewsey and pulled in to gas up at the garage. I went into the store and Sam, the man who ran the store, waited on me. I got a few things and thought, I bet he wonders who this dude is.

He said, "Oh, yeah, you're Don Carlton. You're going up to Glenn Sitz's."

He was friendly and asked if I was going to buckaroo with Glenn. I told him I was.

He said, "Well, you'll have some lumps in your saddle before you get back."

I laughed. He kidded me a little bit.

I bought eight dollars worth of groceries and started to pay for them.

He said, "Hey, it'll be handier if you just charge that and pay me for everything when you leave."

I hadn't heard anything like that in the last fifteen years. I took my sack of groceries and went back to the garage where they were filling my rig with gas. I met Alan Williams who ran the garage and post office. He made me feel at home. Alan and Sissy, his wife, have become my good friends over the years.

I was a little nervous, going in where I did not know a soul. My whole entree was through my friend, Guy Marshall. I thought, gee whiz, here I am a greenhorn. I'll probably be in their way.

We drove on across the river—the Middle Fork of the Malheur River goes right through Drewsey—and went north into Otis Valley. It is a beautiful valley with several ranches in it. Guy had drawn me a map. I could see where Rod Robertson lived. His ranch joined his dad's—the Bill Robertson ranch. I passed the Beulah Reservoir Road, which went by the Edmundson ranch and the Altenose ranch. I came to a set of corrals and stock scales. This was the main Robertson ranch where Bill and Carol Robertson lived. I could look over and see, according to my map, Glenn Sitz's ranch.

I turned onto a dirt road going into the Sitz ranch. Guy had described it for me—a green ranch house overlooking hay fields. Antelope grazed between where we were and where the valley started turning into hills.

This was the high mountain desert country of Oregon. It is mostly sagebrush and juniper all the way from Bend, through Burns and on into Drewsey. From Drewsey on north into the Otis Valley, you head into the mountains. Further up, the terrain gets rough and rocky, treed with some terrific pine forests. The country is wide open, without underbrush. It has some straight up places and some straight down places. If that country was ironed out, it would probably cover half of the United States.

We drove very slowly over rough road up to Glenn's gate, opened it and went in. It was the gate Guy had told me about, made out of horseshoes welded together.

This had been a long trip. We had spent the night before on the Metolius River close to Sisters where we made camp on Canyon Creek. It had a good place to make a picket line for my horse.

That morning I had gotten up and ridden a little to give Rusty some exercise. The ride also took a little of the jump out of him.

At Glenn's I found a level place to park the trailer. There wasn't a soul at the ranch. Grace set up housekeeping in our trailer. I unloaded Rusty, put him in one of the several big corrals they had there and threw him some of the hay I had brought along for him.

Eventually Bridget Sitz, whose nickname was Bridgie, drove in. I hadn't met any of these people so I was hesitant to come in cold like that. But Bridgie was so nice to us that it smoothed the way perfectly. She invited us into the ranch house.

Pretty soon Glenn came in. He was very hospitable. We had dinner with them that night and got acquainted. We felt like we had known them for years.

Glenn was a few years older than I. He was not a big man, maybe five ten or five eleven and weighed one hundred eighty pounds. I will always remember that Glenn was a big eater. He must have worked it off, though. He didn't have an ounce of fat on him. He had about the bluest eyes I have ever seen.

Glenn's dad was a rancher and Glenn grew up ranching. He ranched because he loved the life, and he worked very hard to sustain it.

Glenn's brother, Jim Sitz, had a big ranch up the Malheur River from Drewsey about twelve or fourteen miles from Glenn's place. There were quite a few Sitzes around.

Glenn had several hundred deeded acres on his ranch and also allotments around the ranch that he leased from the Bureau of Land Management. The next three days we would go out on the BLM allotments, gather cattle and sort them. He wanted to take the biggest, strongest calves, the oldest calves, up on the mountain.

Glenn had a Forest Service allotment in the mountains where he had permits for about two hundred fifty pairs or units. He paid an allotment price for each unit. A unit is a cow and a calf. He took the cattle up to the mountains on June 1, and took them out on September 30.

Lindsay Hall, a ranch hand on Glenn's ranch, was about sixty. He was a slight guy, weighing around one hundred forty pounds. Lindsay had been a cowboy all his life. He had been born in a cave close to Drewsey and had spent his early life around Drewsey. The fingers on his hands were so crippled that they went in different directions. He knew cows and was good help.

Lindsay had some horses he was proud of and wanted me to

see. I walked out to the pasture with him, probably three quarters of a mile, to catch them.

On the way we stopped to see a big Appaloosa stallion that he kept in one of the corrals. The horse had rolled on some rocks and had a bad wound on his withers that had festered and was dirty.

I told Lindsay, "Gee, Lindsay, if we don't do something with that wound, it is going to cause you some real trouble."

He said, "Well, I haven't got anything."

I told him I did. I said, "You catch that stud and I'll doctor it."

I got some warm water out of the trailer. We washed the wound. I had Furasin cream mixed half and half with DMSO that Brent Milleson, my veterinarian, had given me. It is about half greasy and is very good on an open sore that can't be bandaged.

We put that on. It bit in a little bit. By the time I left the ranch a week later, the stud was well on his way to healing. I left Lindsay with enough medicine to take care of the wound.

Lindsay came in one day. He had been working on a fence. He talked in a big gravely voice. He said, "Guess what I saw today. I got off my horse and went to open the gate and there was Mr. rattlesnake right there all coiled up and buzzing at me."

I said, "What did you do?"

He said, "Ah, I flung my hammer at him and killed that son of a bitch." He said, "Here, I brought these for you."

He gave me a set of rattles. He was so proud of them. I still have those rattles on my bookcase. I have two or three rattlesnake rattles that all came from Lindsay.

Lindsay thought I was about the nicest guy in the world, helping him with his horse, giving him the medicine. He wanted to pay me back for helping him. During the next few days, he also tried to explain what I was doing wrong or right to help me.

That first day we gathered cattle around the northwest part of the ranch. It was Glenn and Lindsay and Sherri, Glenn's granddaughter, and me. My horse, Rusty, took to the cows right off. He was nervous at first, but settled in.

Glenn took a look at Rusty and said, "Don, you won't see any horses that good on this ranch. He's a good looking son of a gun. Where did you find a horse like that?"

That made me feel good. Rusty was the best horse I ever owned and I have had a lot of them. He was good looking and well reined. He had courage. He would do whatever I wanted him to do.

Rusty also had a lot of spirit and spunk. This was May 27 and it was freezing every night. We had breakfast about five in the ranch house and left there about six. It would still be freezing. Rusty wasn't used to those cold mornings and he had a little hump in his back. I was pretty careful for about half an hour until he warmed up.

The first morning, on our way up to Glenn's reservoir, a big reservoir about three or four miles above his house, I asked Glenn, "You got any rattlesnakes around here?"

He said, "Don, this is where rattlesnakes started. There's quite a few, but I've never been bitten by one. Once in awhile a horse gets bitten and it might make him sick a little. But a horse is big enough so the poison doesn't kill him. Now and then we get a dog rattlesnake bit and once in awhile it will kill them. Just watch your step and you'll be all right."

I, like most people, do not like snakes. I thought, boy, I'll watch for those. But I got so interested in what we were doing and was having so much fun that I don't think I had rattlesnakes on my mind for even five minutes longer.

This was an excuse to do what I loved to do—ride horseback in the outdoors, in the wide open country. We saw deer and antelope every day and a coyote or two. We did see and kill a few rattlesnakes now and then.

Gathering cattle was new to me. When you gather them, you try not to pick up a loose calf. But now and then a calf will be alone, especially an older calf. Maybe the cow has gone for water.

I did not know that to start with and I picked up a lone calf and drove it toward the herd. Then I saw Glenn come over the hill driving it back. When I saw the calf coming, Rusty and I rode out and drove it back toward Glenn. Glenn waved his arms. He said, "Hey, the mother is not with that calf; we want it to go back to where it came from."

That was my first lesson. I rode over to Glenn and said, "Now whatever you do, don't hesitate to tell me when I make a mistake. I don't want to come up here and just ride. I want to help you."

None of those ranchers up there like to say, "You do this and you do that." You have to learn almost by yourself because they don't want to tell you anything that might hurt your feelings.

Glenn told me that the only way you can tell when a cow and a calf are a pair—a mother and baby—is when the calf nurses, called "mothering up," or if a cow licks a calf. Even though a calf might go stand by a cow, you can't jump to conclusions. The mother

Glenn Sitz gathering cattle near Drewsey.

will smell the calf and if it's her calf, she'll let it nurse. If it's not her calf, she will kick that little calf halfway to Sunday to get it out of there. If a cow reaches out and starts licking a calf, you can bet your shoes that calf belongs to her. This was new to me. I wondered at the rules and mysteries of nature.

We took the bunch we had to a fence corner where they were easy to hold. In a fence corner, one or two riders can hold a bunch of cattle. The cows were bawling and the calves were looking for their mothers. As the pairs mothered up, they quieted down. Glenn cut out the pairs. We were there an hour or so before they all mothered up.

I did not attempt to pick out any pairs in that herd. Sherri and I held the cattle. Sherri, who was about eight years old, was a good cowgirl. I am sure she was better help than I was because I was learning. She knew what was going on and she was a good rider. She took her old mare any place. She went up the steepest places I ever saw to get a wandering cow or calf.

We wound up with two or three cows running back and forth bawling, looking for their calves. Their calves were probably back where we first picked up the cows, so Glenn turned them loose.

I said, "Glenn, how in the world is that cow going to find its calf?"

Glenn said, "That cow will go back to the spot where the calf last nursed, and the calf will go back there, too."

I said, "You've got to be kidding!"

He said, "No, sometimes when you're driving cattle a long way, you'll maybe take a cow five miles away from its calf. As soon as she gets free, she'll go back. And she'll go back through all the rough country or through whatever it takes to get back to that spot where she last nursed."

To me that was a wonderful rule of how Mother Nature takes care of her own. That little old calf might be only six or eight weeks old and it'll go find its mother.

We gathered cattle all morning and sorted them. Glenn picked the biggest, strongest calves and all that had been branded. We put the new ones that hadn't been branded in a different pasture. Along toward afternoon, we started driving them toward the ranch. We had anywhere from twenty to thirty head and had them in one bunch.

One thing that became very clear to me was how important two riders are in gathering cattle. One rider can easily handle a pair—one cow and one calf—but has his hands full with two pair. If one pair splits off and goes down one side of the canyon and the other pair goes the other way, the rider has to follow one pair or the other.

Two riders can handle thirty head pretty easy. One rider stays in the drag to keep them moving. The other rider keeps them from straying. One rider is going to be pretty busy at times, especially when the cattle are being driven away from green grass and they don't want to go.

One time Rod Robertson and I moved seven hundred yearlings for quite a ways, just the two of us. But that was a big handful and we normally didn't do that.

When we got back that evening, Grace had fixed dinner in our trailer. Bridgie and Glenn ate dinner with us that night. Grace and Bridgie hit it off from the word go. Grace was born and raised on a farm in Tennessee. Bridgie had grown up on a ranch and was a rancher's wife.

The next morning after breakfast in the ranch house, Glenn, Lindsay, Sherri and I headed for Cottonwood Basin where he had a bigger bunch of cattle. We did the same thing we had done the day before.

We gathered up a bunch and found a fence corner. I held them. Glenn cut out the pairs as they mothered up and drove them through an open gate that headed down toward the ranch. This took us pretty much all day.

We came back and had a short cocktail hour and then dinner with Glenn and Bridgie. I asked Bridgie at dinner that night, "Bridgie, are you from Drewsey, too? Did you grow up here?"

She said, "Oh, no, I'm from over at Lightning Creek."

I asked her where Lightning Creek was. Well, Lightning Creek was only about twenty-five miles away. The two of them, she and Glenn, had been in that country around Burns all their lives.

The third day we rode to Cottonwood Basin again. Philip Sitz, Glenn's nephew, helped us. We rounded up more cattle and cut out enough to make two hundred and fifty pairs.

We drove those pairs back and put them in with the others we had cut out the day before. Then we drove all of them back to the ranch and put them in the lane. The lane is along the road and is about two or three miles long. It has grass and water. Cottonwood Creek flows through there.

That afternoon we gathered up ten bulls to put in the bunch. They figure on one bull for twenty-five cows. Everything was ready to go.

I had been there three days, working with cattle around that ranch. By now I had learned a little bit. I still had a lot to learn, but it was soaking in. I learned that a lot of things you see in the movies you flat do not do.

Number one, you never run the cows and calves unless you have to. Now and then you have to when one tries to get away.

Maybe you have to rope a calf. But the ranchers want that fat on the stock to stay there. They do not want them excited. They work around them very easy.

When we held cattle in the fence corners and the ranchers cut out pairs, they didn't do it like you see in the cutting horse shows. In those shows they take one steer or heifer out of a herd and put it up against a fence and let it try to get back to the herd. The more action, the better.

On a ranch they let the cattle quiet down. They let the pairs mother up. Then they ride in slowly, pick out a pair, get between them and the others, and push them out of the herd. Now and then the cow and calf get excited and start running to get back to the herd. Once in awhile they lose them back in the herd. But it is all done slowly and quietly.

I learned that if it was a cool day, the cattle moved along well. If was a hot day, along toward afternoon they wanted to shade up. If there weren't enough of them to string out, it was important to keep the bunch together where we could see them

We finished gathering the cattle that day. We made plans to move the cattle to the Forest Service allotment the next day. The first half of the day we would go up Squaw Creek Road, an old, two-rut gravel road. If two pickups met on this road, one would have to stop and pull over to let the other one go by. The road led up to the Forest Reserve Line, where we would leave BLM land and go into Forest Service land—about eleven miles from the ranch.

The fourth morning we had breakfast at the ranch at four. What a breakfast. Lord! We had bacon and sausage and eggs and hot cakes and hot cereal and black coffee.

Every day I had been in Drewsey, the weather had gotten a little warmer, although we still had ice in the water buckets in the morning. We were around four thousand feet in elevation.

We saddled up and went out to the lane where we had put the cows and calves. It was a little after five. Six riders were taking the cattle up: Glenn Sitz, Sherri Sitz, Philip Sitz, Walter Sitz, who was another of Glenn's nephews and the ramrod of the drive that day, Lindsay Hall and me.

One of the Sitz boys rode up to the far end and opened the gate. The rest of us started the cattle. They strung out for about a quarter of a mile. Then we started up the hill. We were trying to make the Forest Reserve line by noon.

Cows pretty much set their own speed. The old cows in the

herd who had been to the mountains before, and there were always more old cows than new ones, knew the way and where they were going. We got them strung out so they were moving along well. This was the ideal time to move cattle—early in the morning.

We had been on the road maybe an hour when we came to one place where the road curved in a bit. Because it was so steep, the fence dropped down the hill and went straight so there was no fence to hold the cattle on the road.

A big old rugged Hereford cow can go just about any place she wants to go. It doesn't make any difference how steep down or how steep up, she gets there one way or another. When we got to that place in the road, about eighty percent of that bunch of cows went about one hundred yards down that real steep hill. It took half an hour for us to get them milled out of that corner and going up the road again.

I said to myself, here I am at my heart's delight. I'm a cowboy! Here I am with all these bawling cattle going uphill. We were headed for the mountains and we were traveling real good.

Little did I realize that young calves get tired. These calves were a couple of months old; some not more than a month old.

As we got up into Squaw Creek, we got into some tough places. Every now and then some of the cows tried to ditch the riders to get away. They ran up steep banks and went into thick scrub oak or tight brush.

Oh, brother, now it was work. I wondered if my horse could get in some of those places. On the real bad places I let Walt and Philip, the cowboys, do the work until I learned how to get in there. They had to go into some bad bad places. But we couldn't lose any of the cattle. They were worth too much money.

Every once in a while we came to a place where the fence was close on both sides and the cattle were going good. At these times, the cowboys and I would get off our horses and walk for ten minutes. It really helped the legs and helped keep us from getting sore.

We passed the road leading to Guy Marshall's cabin just three miles before the Forest Reserve Line. It was remote.

By noon we were at the Forest Reserve Line. It was a welcome sight. My rump was getting a little bit tired and my legs were getting a little bit sore. I knew I had been some place.

We ran the cattle into one end of a big corral, then ran them through a chute. The Forest Service man counted each cow and sprayed its rear end with red paint. The paint stayed on a long time. He didn't count the calves. The rancher was paying on every cow-calf unit that was brought to the allotment.

After the cattle were counted, we drove them across the road to a holding pen of maybe five acres. It had a reservoir in the middle of it so the cows could drink.

While we were still running the cows through the chute, another herd of cattle came up the east side of Squaw Creek fence. We had come up the west side. These were the Robertsons: Bill and Carol, their two sons Rod and Rex, and their wives Debbie and Rose. I hadn't met these people.

I got off my horse and was stretching. Bill rode up. He had a pipe in his mouth. He took the pipe out and said, "The saddle got a few lumps in it?"

I said, "Boy, it has. It's got more right now than when I started at five this morning."

He laughed and said, "Yeah, that's right."

I pulled my saddle off Rusty to give his back a rest.

Bridgie and Grace arrived with lunch. Bridgie was driving Glenn's big stock truck, which had room for five horses. Grace was driving my truck for my horse.

I thought we might be going back to the ranch, but then it looked to me like we might be going further than this because of the big lunch.

In the back of her truck Bridgie had a paper towel box about two feet high and three feet square. It was full. It had a baked ham, huge amounts of potato salad, bread, candy bars and other fixings. We had a banquet right there at the Forest Service corral.

The Robertsons had lunch with us. They were going northeast of the Reserve line corral. We were going northwest.

They were waiting for us to get out of the corral so the Forest Service man could count their cattle, paint them and get them ready to go on. We were on the ground an hour. After the beautiful lunch, I was tired. I thought, Boy! I hope we don't have to go much further.

Up to now I had been on horseback seven hours, which was the longest I had ever been in the saddle. I had been on some long rides and maybe seven hours or more in a day, but not that long in one stretch.

I was green as a gourd. I had no idea where we were going and not too sure where we were.

We got back in our saddles. We shook our bunch of cows, calves and bulls out of the holding lot and started them again. We had gone up the road not even a quarter of a mile when Glenn rode up ahead and turned the herd straight west. We headed off the road then and up a steep hill. We broke over the rim and looked down into the most beautiful valley I think I have ever seen. It was Antelope Swale. Antelope Peak was to the right of us.

The Swale was owned by Gerald Allen, a rancher. I could see way down to about the middle of the swale, at least five miles away, to a line cabin with a metal roof. A pickup truck sat by the cabin. There were horses in a holding lot next to a pasture.

I thought, "Well, this is evidently where we're going with these cows."

We headed down with the five hundred head of cattle. We were moving at the most two miles an hour and the cows and calves were not going in a straight line. We were constantly riding out to the side to bring a cow back. I am sure all of us rode at least twenty-five miles on that eleven mile trip up the mountain that morning because of those side excursions.

By the time we got to the bottom of Antelope Swale, we hit a fence, which was very welcome. That fence was like having six more cowboys because we could push the cattle up against the fence to hold them as we moved them.

We took turns getting off our horses and walking to rest a bit. Three of us would get off and walk at a time.

By then I was beginning to wonder. I got back on my horse and rode up beside Walt and said, "Hey, Walt, where are we going with these cows?"

He looked at me kind of funny. He said, "Don, do you see up there on the horizon?" He pointed out a ways.

I said, "Yeah."

He said, "There's a spring up there called Westfall Springs. There's another line camp up there, which is our line camp. It's called Bluebucket Cow Camp." He said, "We'll ride up there on the other side of Gerald Allen's cabin. We'll cut in there and go in through Bluebucket, through the horse pasture and holding lots there. Then we'll go on up past Moffit Springs and Bear Springs."

I didn't have the heart to ask him how much farther it was. By now it was about four in the afternoon. Grace and Bridgie were meeting us at Westfall Springs.

We got to Bluebucket, a beautiful old line camp, and kept on going. We broke out onto an old road and started the herd up that

Bluebucket Cow Camp sits in the mountains above Drewsey, Oregon.

road. It was a Forest Service road and the Forest Service had been through there cutting slash.

Cutting slash means thinning pine trees. The pines grow too thick for the amount of rain they get a year. So the Forest Service goes through and cuts out most of the young jackpine stuff and lets it fall. They come through later, stack it and burn it.

They hadn't gathered or stacked the slash yet. They had just gone through with chainsaws. The jackpines were about four inches in diameter and from eight to twenty feet tall. Wherever they fell, they just laid.

The sun was hot. The cows and calves were tired and they were hard to push. There were more in the drag by far than there had been that morning. When we came across country, the young calves laid down beside sagebrush. They were easy to miss so riders were constantly riding back and forth looking for these calves.

The slash made it that much harder to keep those cows and calves moving. They would get out in the slash and stop. They were smart. Some of the slash was three or four feet high. We couldn't get our horses into it. So the guys had to go in on foot and run the cattle out. It was hard work.

By now I had been in the saddle ten hours. I thought to myself, "What in the hell are you doing, Don. You're worn out; you probably won't make it. They might have to bury you here. You are growing to this saddle. What are you doing here trying to act like a cowboy? You're getting too old for this."

My horse, Rusty, looked at me as if I were nuts. But here I

was. It was certainly no time to change horses and I didn't have a horse to change to if I could. Nobody else did either. So there was nothing to do but finish the job.

It took us about three hours to get through the slash. I didn't think we were going to make it. Even Glenn looked worried. We couldn't leave the cattle. If we did, we would have to ride five thousand acres gathering them up.

It was getting towards seven in the evening and we were still riding. I was about ready to have a convulsion I was so tired. Then there we were at Moffit Springs. I thought, well, Moffit Springs then Bear Springs.

At last we got to Bear Springs and started for Westfall Springs. The cows that had been up there before were in the lead and were eager to get to that good green grass. We were in pine and juniper timber, but without much underbrush. Grace and Bridgie were waiting at Westfall and I could see my white truck for maybe half a mile. I don't think I have ever seen anything that looked so good to me in my whole life as that white truck did.

We got the cows into the springs and everybody quit. The others rode up to Glenn's truck and tied their horses. I rode up to my truck and got off. Grace looked at me. It was nine o'clock. We had started at five that morning. That fifteen hours on horseback was the longest trip I had ever been on.

Grace said, "How are you doing?"

I said, "Well, I made it. I'm here. But I'm tired."

I unsaddled Rusty and cooled him out. Then I rubbed him down. I rubbed his legs with liniment. He stood there with his head down about half asleep. I threw a blanket on him.

The cowboys were eyeing me wondering what the hell I was doing with my horse.

By now I had my coat on. We were at about six thousand feet and it was chilly.

We all had a big lunch again off Bridgie's ham and potato salad. We were there for probably another hour. Then we loaded our horses. I was glad my van was covered. It was cold and Rusty had been through a lot that day.

It was about twenty-two miles back to the ranch. I figured that some of the younger riders—Walt Sitz, Philip Sitz, Sherri, and even Glenn and Lindsay had covered at least seventy miles with the cattle. They rode out to the flanks, then up to the point, then back. I knew I had ridden probably fifty to sixty miles. We hadn't been in a straight line all day.

I didn't say anything, but I was nursing a blister or two. We had ridden quite a bit the day before and I had forgotten to put on boxer shorts instead of jockey shorts. Jockey shorts fit me right where the bones hit the saddle. I had a blister on each side. Before I left that morning, I laid across the bed while Grace put two big patches on my blisters. I took those blisters with me for that fifteen hour ride. Without those patches, I could not have made it.

We got back to the ranch about midnight. I took Rusty into the corral, fed him grain and threw him a nice big bunch of hay. He wasn't interested in eating, but when I got up the next morning, the hay was gone. He had rested up and munched on hay all night.

The next morning he was still tired. I had weighed Rusty at Sisters one time. He weighed twelve hundred ten pounds without his saddle. The saddle, saddle pad and saddlebags probably weighed fifty pounds. I was on top of that. He was a big strong horse but he knew he had been some place. I knew I had, too.

We slept in until about six in the morning. After breakfast we drove back in Glenn's pickup to Westfall Springs to see if the cows had scattered out, and to see if any of them were lame or needed doctoring.

On the way up, we stopped and Grace and I walked up to the ridge that we had gone over the day before. I showed Grace the beautiful view down into Antelope Swale and took pictures of Antelope Swale and the Forest Service corrals. I had planned to take pictures during the cattle drive, but, Lord, I didn't have time. Grace did take some moving pictures the previous day.

We drove around to Bluebucket Cow Camp then on to Moffit Springs and Bear Springs and up to Westfall Springs where we had dropped those five hundred head of cattle. There was not one single cow or calf or bull in sight. They had just scattered.

Of course, it was early in the spring and the grass was growing. The old cows knew what they were up there for and that was to fill up on green grass for three or four months.

They were in the top Forest Service allotment. Glenn and four other ranchers had four allotments together, covering about 20,000 acres. The fences cross right in the middle so they could keep the cattle scattered out or keep them in one area. It was known as the Drewsey Co-op.

The Forest Service is careful that the cattle don't clean out too much grass or mess up the springs. So the Drewsey Co-op

hired a cowboy to stay at the cow camp all summer and ride the
allotment to keep an eye on the cattle.

They were logging in the allotment and the loggers would
leave gates open, so the rider would make sure they were closed.

That day I took more movies at Westfall Springs. These are
old cattle and sheep springs. The springs are not a big force of
water. The Forest Service or rancher had tapped into the spring,
dug it out, put a pipe into it, put gravel around it and screened it.
Out of that pipe runs not more than a gallon of water every two to
five minutes. So they have several hollowed-out logs there to catch
the water. This way one cow couldn't drink all the water. The logs
are evidence that these are old time springs. Bear Springs had
iron tubs with floats on them.

I couldn't get over how long it had taken us to get the cows up
there. I was feeling pretty good, though. I figured the sitting end
of my body was numb. But I wasn't really sore, just tired.

While we ate our picnic lunch, I asked Glenn, "What do you
call a long horseback ride? What's the longest ride you've ever
been on?"

He thought a minute, then said. "Well, I don't know. I guess
the longest one was when I was a kid. We used to go to Burns and
back on horseback in a day."

Burns from the ranch is forty-seven miles. I said, "You mean
to tell me that you rode from the ranch into Burns and then back
in one day?"

He said, "Yeah, we sure did."

I said, "What gait did you ride at?"

He said, "Oh, a trot."

This is one thing you learn up here in this ranch country. If
you have a lot of work to do or if you have a long way to go, the
easiest gait on the horse is a trot. So if you are not going to haul
the horses out to where you're working, and you usually don't if
it's under five miles, you ride out at a trot.

When the ranchers trot, they all post, just like an English
rider does. It's a natural way to ride when you're on a long trot.
But I could not imagine riding ninety-four miles to town and back
at a trot.

In many books I have read, though, such as Reub Long's
Oregon Desert, there are instances of continuous horseback rides
of eighty to one hundred miles.

I always tried to teach my horse that there wasn't any such

gait as a trot. But I am out for strictly pleasure. These ranchers are out to get work done where time is of the essence. So I learned to trot with them.

However, they had never seen a Quarter horse that walked like my horse did. They all marveled that Rusty walked as fast as some of their horses trotted.

After I got to know Glenn better, I said, "You know, Glenn, dadgummit, it looked to me like that was pretty hard on those cows. I'd take those cattle up to the Reserve Line corral holding pen, and let them rest there all night. Then I'd kick them out and take them the rest of the way the next day."

He said, "Yeah, that's what we should have done. This is the first time we've ever taken them all the way and it was just too much in one day. But once we got them out of those holding pens, there wasn't any place else we could have dropped them until we got to where we were."

He said, "I didn't know that slash was going to be down between Bluebucket and Moffit Springs. That really killed us. I didn't see how we were going to get through there, I really didn't. But we had to get through if it took all night."

I learned on this trip that a greenhorn on a cattle drive has to push the cattle, keep them moving. There is always a bunch of cattle in the drag, usually the oldest ones and the slowest ones and the tiredest ones. The rest of them are lined out in front. Those in the drag will try to stop. You have to keep them moving, but you can't push them faster than they want to walk or you get into trouble.

If you push that back end too hard, you push them right up through the middle of the rest of the cattle and you ruin the string. They will not be lined out any more. I have seen this happen with new people. I have been guilty of it myself thinking I was really helping, thinking, how come the rest of those guys don't get in there and work as hard as I do. But that's not the way. The others are waiting for you to learn that you shouldn't do that.

I am not the most patient person and it's pretty hard to lay back when you've been moving cows all day long and they are slowing down. It's hard to not get behind and try to hurry them.

I learned that if it's your first time out and you don't know much about cattle, stay back and watch what the rest of the riders do. If they are people who live there, they pretty much know what they are doing.

Most city people make a real blunder in talking to ranchers, especially cattlemen. Almost always the first question is, "How many cattle do you have?"

That's like the rancher asking me, "Don, how much money do you have in the bank."

I know from experience that the rancher looks on that question being asked of him exactly as I would look at that question being asked of me. This reminds me of a quote in Herman Oliver's book, *Gold and Cattle Country*, where Herman Oliver discusses a similar situation.

He tells of a city fellow stopping on the road watching a herd of cattle being driven by a few cowboys. The city fellow walks over and talks to one of the cowboys and says, "Whose cattle are those?"

The cowboy says, "Feller up the ridge."

The city fellow says, "Where are you taking them?"

The cowboy says, "Over the hump."

The city fellow says, "How many you got here?"

The cowboy says, "Quite a few."

That first trip to Drewsey was in 1972 and I was fifty-seven years old. Well, too old or not, a year later I was headed for Glenn's ranch

On the way to Drewsey, we stopped in the Metolius River area to ride. We camped in a nice meadow with a beautiful spring coming up on the edge of it. The ice cold water flowed down to another creek, which flowed into Canyon Creek, which flowed into the Metolius River.

Bob and Polly Eastman, their son, Casey, Bob and Pat Spring and their sons, Billy and Bobby, met us there. Sid and Sue Nolan came in the next day. Sue had worked for me at Mayflower for many years. That day we rode to Cabot Lake and had lunch.

On May 28 I left for Drewsey. Grace went back home with the Springs. I got into Glenn's ranch about five thirty that evening. It was still early in the year for that country and it was chilly when the sun went down.

We had the same people: Glenn Sitz, his granddaughter, Sherri Sitz, his two nephews, Walt and Philip Sitz, the hired man Lindsay Hall, and me.

On May 30 we all went into Drewsey for the big Memorial Day potluck dinner in the Grange Hall. We cleaned graves and put out flowers in the Drewsey cemetery. Then we had a roping contest with Mexican steers to head and heel.

On May 31 we got up at five a.m. and spent the rest of the day rounding up and sorting the cattle that were going to the mountains. Glenn had started the process earlier in the week and we finished it on the 31st.

On Friday, June 1, we got up at four in the morning. After a big breakfast we left the ranch about five. We still had ice in the buckets and around mud puddles.

We headed the cattle straight up the mountain. The Forest Service had dropped the practice of checking each rancher into the Forest Service and painting the cattle. So we didn't go through the Forest Service corrals. That saved us about five or six miles. We cut off the Drewsey Road at Ice Box Canyon, then went across country up over a ridge and down into Antelope Swale.

This meant we didn't have a closed pasture to run the cattle into and sit down for lunch like we had the year before. We ate our lunch in the saddle. During the time I ate one sandwich and four cookies, I had to stop eating and chase at least six critters that were trying to get away from the herd.

We got to cow camp about five that night. Bridget had a big dinner there for us to enjoy. There is nothing that makes a person hungrier than being outside.

After that second trip, I could not see how cattle could be raised on a big scale without horses and cowboys and long days. In that eighteen miles or so Glenn must have ridden at least one hundred miles. The young cowboys must have covered at least eighty-five miles, and I think I covered at least sixty miles.

None of our riding was in a straight line. It was straight ahead, then out to the right, then straight ahead, then out to the left, then back to pick up a stray, always riding away from the straight line.

I was much more help to Glenn this time than the year before.

At the end of my second spring trip to help Glenn Sitz move cattle, he told me that the best riding is in the fall. The five ranchers who used the Bluebucket grazing area had to be out of the Forest Service land by the first part of October. They had to gather the cattle off 25,000 or so acres, which meant every rider was important. Glenn told me the cowboys would go up and spend about ten days at Bluebucket Cow Camp riding out each morning to gather cattle.

Glenn said, "You'd really enjoy the riding. We usually don't get out until about nine. We wait until the cattle gather at the waterholes in the mid-morning."

As Glenn described it to me, I knew I was going to have to try it. That fall of 1973 I took a week's vacation and skinned out early on Friday. My trailer was ready. I had hay and feed loaded for my horse and all my gear. I got home, changed clothes, loaded Rusty into the truck, hooked up the trailer, kissed Grace good-bye and took off for Bluebucket Cow Camp above Drewsey.

I went over the Cascade Mountains and spent the night on Canyon Creek in the Metolius River area. I pulled in just before dark and made camp. I unloaded Rusty and made him comfortable. I fed him, then fixed myself a steak and went to bed early.

I got up at dawn the next morning, fed Rusty and fixed my breakfast with half a dozen cups of coffee. I settled back and enjoyed the absolute beauty of that country and the smell of it. The smell alone is worth the trip.

I loaded up and drove to Burns and called Glenn. That spring he had told me a short cut to Bluebucket. I went through Buchanan and took the cut off at the Pine Creek Road and followed Bluebucket Road to the cow camp, about eighteen miles.

Bluebucket Cow Camp sits right on the western edge of Antelope Swale, which is a great huge place. It's two inches wide

The old cabin at Bluebucket Cow Camp.

on a big map. It's straight across country from the Forest Service corrals, probably five miles and that's not around by road.

Small pine timber and juniper trees and sagebrush grow right around the cabin. Down behind and east of the cabin are big holding lots.

The Bluebucket Cow Camp was strictly a line camp. The cabin used by the people in the Drewsey Co-op was rustic. It had two rooms—a bedroom and a kitchen. An old wood range and a big table and chairs sat in the kitchen.

They never locked the door. They always had wood in the woodbox inside and matches in case somebody got caught out in bad weather. It was a place to get in out of storms.

The first time I went up there, old pictures hung on its walls. Some of these pictures were fifty or more years old, keepsakes of the people who owned the cabin.

Shortly after that year, things started to disappear out of the cabin. Most people who go up into the hills are good, honest, nice people. But there's always some son-of-a-gun who has sticky fingers, who feels like the people who are trying to be good to him, who leave the cabin open so he can use it, also mean for him to pick up some of their almost-priceless little things.

So the owners had to clean out the cabin because some thief couldn't keep his hands off what didn't belong to him. I guess that's our changing times. It is one change that is certainly not for the better.

No one was at Bluebucket, but it had a nice camp with corrals for the horses. I made a picket line for Rusty. I strung a rope twenty feet from one tree to another. I had a four-inch steel ring on the rope and I tied Rusty's halter rope to that steel ring. This gave him room to maneuver back and forth and didn't keep his head tied right square up to the tree where he might paw out the roots. I put a ten-by-twelve-foot tarp over a rope and strung it to the

Rusty tied to the horse van at Bluebucket Cow Camp.

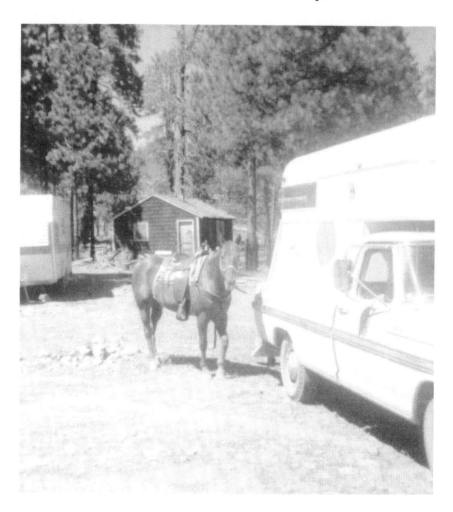

trees as a roof over Rusty. In case the weather got bad, he could get under it.

Everybody always kidded me about how I took care of my horse, but I know he appreciated it. A horse is an outdoor animal and he is used to the weather. If it's real cold, a loose horse runs back and forth to keep warm. But when he's tied up, he can't run. So I always fixed a shelter for my horse. I had a canvas tarp and special poles for it.

I set up camp with my twenty-one-foot Terry vacation trailer on the off side of the horse corrals. I tried the water from the Bluebucket Springs and found the coldest, nicest water I ever tasted. The water is piped from the springs to the cabin where it flows into a large tank where the horses drink. The cabin doesn't have any running water in it so we caught water in a bucket for personal use.

Glenn Sitz came by and said the ranchers would be up the next morning. Glenn stuck around and we shot the breeze for awhile. After he left, I fixed a steak dinner on a little Hibachi barbecue that I had brought along. I got to bed early. I was waiting with great anticipation for the next morning.

The ranchers drove up the next morning about nine. Most of them had two horses. They turned the horses they weren't riding that day into the pasture. The horse pasture was about five hundred acres. That night they turned all the horses out except a wrangle horse, which they kept in the corral. This gave them one horse in the morning to bring in the other horses.

Each morning, one of the younger ranchers saddled the wrangle horse and rode out. He was back in twenty or thirty minutes with the whole bunch of horses and ran them into the corral. They all picked the horses they were going to ride that day, led them out, saddled them up and loaded them into the truck.

They didn't understand why I didn't turn my horse out with their horses. My experience told me he would be picked on because he was the strange horse. He would get skinned up, maybe even get kicked and get a leg broken. So I never turned my horse in with strange horses. I always found a corral or put up a picket line where I could keep my horse separate.

The ranchers who belonged to the Drewsey Co-op were Tom Howard, Tom's son, Tom Howard, Jr., known as Tommy, Byron Dunten and his son, Charles, Floyd Dunten and his son, Steve, Lloyd Jordan, and, of course, Lindsay Hall, Glenn's right-hand man. I had met most of these men at the Memorial Day goings on earlier in the year.

We loaded the horses into the stock trucks and hauled about fifteen miles to the far end of the grazing allotment. We went down through Lake Camp toward Logan Valley and Strawberry Mountain. We were between Burns and Prairie City, Oregon, in the foothills around the mountains at about six thousand feet. The days were warm and nice, but the nights were cold.

We unloaded the horses and tied our slickers on behind our saddles. In the mountains in the Northwest, you never leave without a slicker on the back of your saddle regardless of how the weather looks. The mountains get a lot of thunderstorms. I have been in some hummers.

That first day was beautiful. I was completely at my heart's delight. This is what I had wanted to do for the last fifty-eight years. Everyone made over my horse, which made me feel good.

They didn't say a whole lot, but they took a good look at Rusty, walked around him quietly. I knew enough about horses to know they had to have liked what they saw. Rusty was a big strong Quarter horse with a big strong rear end, big gaskin muscles and a good head. He was a sorrel without white.

As we were riding along, a cowboy and I had eight or ten pairs of cows and calves in front of us on an old dirt road. The cows were going well. Derrick Carpenter, a young cowboy, was eyeing Rusty. I was holding Rusty in so he wouldn't outwalk the other horses and make them uncomfortable.

Derrick said, "You know, Don, we're going to have to upgrade our horses here in Drewsey."

We drove the cattle we gathered in a day through Bluebucket Camp and down about a mile into the edge of Antelope Swale to the holding pastures. There was enough feed and water in the pastures to hold the cattle until we were ready to separate them and drive them to the ranch. On some days we gathered a hundred head of cattle, on others thirty. It just depended on luck.

Each cow and calf had a brand, ear mark and dewlap. The ear marks were of all kinds. A swallowfork on the right ear might be one rancher's ear mark. The ear marks are registered and listed with each rancher's brand. The dewlap is a marking on the brisket, which lets some skin grow out of the brisket and hang down. How far it hangs down is one mark. Calves are branded, marked and dewlapped early in the spring when they are two weeks to two months old.

These ranchers can tell their own cows from far away. I never could. I'm still going up there and I've gotten close enough to see the brand before I knew whose cow it was by the dewlap or ear mark.

On the second day out Glenn said, "Don, let's you and me take Black Canyon on the way back."

I said, "Fine with me, Glenn."

I noticed Charles Dunten looked at Walt Sitz and they both kind of smiled.

I thought, well, I bet I'm getting into something here.

We did go to Black Canyon and we did get into something. Black Canyon is well named. It is black and big and steep. It is dark because of the underbrush. There isn't much underbrush in this country, but there was a lot of downed stuff in the canyon. We got down to the bottom and rode around through the bottom of it.

Glenn said, "We don't find too many cattle in here but there are always a few pairs. It's real rough. We might have to lead our horses a ways."

He was right. About the time we got into Black Canyon, I had to get off Rusty because we could not get under the brush. There was one place where I had to unsaddle Rusty to get him under the downfall. I dragged the saddle under the downfall and saddled him again.

About lunch we came up out of Black Canyon with a few head. Like Glenn said, there weren't many down there because it was real rough, but there were some down there. We had cows and calves and a bull or two out in front of us. We had to be sure they were pairs—a cow and calf that belonged to each other. If they weren't, we could end up with a calf separated from its mother and have to drive it back ten or twelve miles.

So we periodically stopped at a fence corner or beside a fence where riders could hold the cattle, and let them mother up. If there was a cow or calf in the bunch that didn't belong, we turned it back. Of course, it wasn't hard to turn the cow or calf back because it was trying to get out.

Sometimes in a big bunch, the calf can't find its mother. It gets excited and wants to go back, but its mother is up at the other end of the bunch. It takes a lot of understanding, and this is the place for a greenhorn to sit back and watch. When a calf is nursing, you know it is that calf's mother. But to decide that the mother of this calf over here is not in this group of sixty head is a decision I would just as soon the person who owns the calf make.

If an old cow has a tight bag, one that hasn't been nursed for awhile, then there's a calf out there somewhere. Maybe the calf is dead, but it is missing and you should leave the cow right there. Most of the calves have been on those cows all summer and the cows are pretty well dried up so their bags are not like a milk cow's. At that time of year it's hard to tell a dry range cow from one who is being nursed by a calf. You have to be careful.

We stopped for lunch at Westfall Springs and I lost my good jackknife. I was cutting up something or other, took it out and set it on a stump. I never did find it although I went back to that stump and looked.

After lunch we picked up and drove the cattle again along the old dirt roads back towards Bluebucket Cow Camp. I was the new man so I was delegated to help drive the cows. Two or three of us always drove the cattle while the others gathered.

After we got the cattle back to camp, we built a campfire and had a cocktail or two. We talked about the day, talked about the cattle we had missed. Then the ranchers left for home. I fixed my dinner and went to bed.

Each morning we started at the far end of the allotment and rode to every watering hole and spring on all those acres. We scoured every inch of land. Otherwise we could have missed some. Cows and calves separate. Many times we found one pair by themselves or two pair by themselves. A bunch of horses stay together; cows don't.

We didn't ride up to the edge of a real bad place where it looked like it couldn't be traveled by horseback and say, "Well, I hope nothing is down there and leave." We went down into it. If it was too rough, we walked and led our horses. Some way or other we had to get through that country.

That's one of the reasons I think cattle ranching will always take a cowboy and a horse. There is nothing motorized on earth that's going to cover that kind of tough country.

One night we got back and were sitting around the fire. About that time the Eastern Oregon papers had carried several stories about cattle found dead. They thought a freak cult like the Manson group had been there. Some questionable groups of people had been sighted. So the ranchers had been talking about this and they had found several dead cattle. They said their private parts had been cut out. Some had seen a bull that this happened to.

A good bull is worth twelve hundred to twenty-five hundred dollars. When you lose a bull, you really lose something. So the ranchers had been keeping an eye out.

It was a beautiful clear night. It seemed like I could see every star in the universe. When that moon came up, it was almost as bright as day. I never pulled a blind when I was in the trailer. I liked to look out and see everything.

The coyotes always howled and I loved to hear them. But when I'm alone, it's a somewhat eerie feeling. After the cult talk, I was feeling especially alone after the ranchers left. I thought about cows being killed, private parts being cut out and so on.

I went to bed and then woke up. It sounded like eight or ten

Byron Dunten and Glenn Sitz stop to let the cattle mother up on the fall cattle drive.

coyotes were under my trailer and they were really singing. My spine turned to ice and the chills ran up and down it. I couldn't see anything moving. With that moon so bright, it was like daylight. I reached over and put my hand on my revolver and shook it loose from the holster, as if that would do any good.

I wished I had had my tape recorder there so I could have recorded that song that bunch of coyotes were singing to me.

I think that night would have affected most anybody that way. You wake up, You're all alone. You're way up in the hills. And here are those coyotes singing to beat the band. I don't think it would have bothered me if it hadn't been for the story about the dead cattle. But it really gave me a thrill.

Every day that fall we saw animals while we rode. That first year we had a lot of buck deer around and, of course, a lot of does, and a big coyote or two. Every day we came on fresh elk sign and once in awhile we saw one from a distance. We saw one bear. Since then I have seen a bear every year and up to three bears, most of those when I was on horseback.

Many times you can ride up on wild animals horseback, especially if there is just one or two people. They are not as afraid of the four-footed approach as they are to the strange sounds a man makes walking.

One morning we were at Lake Camp and were just starting to gather cattle when the dogs spotted a badger. It was the first badger I had seen alive and not in a zoo. That badger wasn't afraid of us or the horses or the dogs.

We had seven or eight cow dogs. It's almost imperative to have good cow dogs when you're moving or looking for cattle, although some dogs can ruin an hour's worth of work if they are untrained. A cow dog can get into brush where a horse or a man can't go. And it seems like a cow or a calf can get into some of the damnedest places in this whole world and they're hard to get out.

The dogs wanted to get to the badger. The badger backed up to a rock and stood there, waiting for them to come in. He growled and snarled and showed claws that could rip a dog's insides out.

A badger is a vicious little killer. He has a hide on his back that's very loose. Dogs can grab hold of it and shake him but they can't hurt him. They chew him up but his hide is thick and tough. His claws are so sharp and his legs so strong he can dig out of sight within a minute just on flat ground. If a badger gets into you with those claws, look out.

Ranchers are pretty tough on badgers, and for good reason. Badgers dig holes. If you are chasing a cow on a horse and the horse steps in a badger hole, you are apt to take a bad spill and the horse is apt to break his leg. And cows occasionally break a leg in a badger hole. So the ranchers kill a badger if they run onto one, simply to keep the holes down.

We were afraid this badger might kill one of the dogs. So Charles Dunten roped him and dragged him off a ways. I heard the badger hit the end of that rope and growl and snarl. Then Tommy Howard roped him so they had two lariats on the badger. They strung him out between the two horses, spread-eagled. We wanted to kill him but nobody had a gun. He was fighting hard. Finally Charles Dunten got off and killed him with a big rock. He almost got bitten two or three times doing that.

I had my movie camera that day and filmed the badger sequence.

During that week, Lindsay Hall took his pickup into Burns to have some work done on it. All the young cowboys kidded and teased Lindsay in a good natured way. He growled around about it but he loved it.

This one morning when Lindsay didn't show up, Glenn said Lindsay was bringing his own truck and horse trailer. He was bringing up a new colt he wanted to get started.

Pretty soon we heard a vehicle coming. It sounded like an airplane. It was a pickup without a muffler. It was roaring and backfiring now and then. Lindsay drove in pulling the trailer with his colt in it. Tommy and Charles were kidding Lindsay about what he had gotten done to his truck.

Charles Dunten asked, "Lindsay, what happened to your truck? Why does it make so much noise?"

Lindsay said, in his real gravely voice, "Well, I'll tell you. I think they got the muffler too fer back."

Charles said, "Yeah, it's so fer back, I think they left it all the way back in Burns."

One time Lindsay was working on his pickup, putting some oil into it. Charles Dunten sneaked up behind him and tied one foot to the bumper. Lindsay turned around to go and here he was tied tight.

He said, "Oh, you damn kids, you ought to work as hard as you play. You'd get more done."

We rode and gathered cattle every day. As the week wore on, there were fewer cattle left out in those thousands of acres. Some of the old cows liked that freedom and they worked pretty hard at staying away from us.

An old range cow that's been out in the mountains and knows the country gets pretty doggone wily. They are as hard to catch as deer. The ones that stay out the longest are usually those that can hide. So those last few days we had to hunt hard. We had to ride the same places—Black Canyon included—every single day.

All the ranchers knew how many cattle they had on the allotment and they counted them every day as we brought them in. By the end of the gather, it's rare to have all the cattle. There'll be a few pairs missed and almost always some bulls. At that time of year, the bulls get off to themselves, usually two together. If there are three, two run the third one off. But two buddy up and sometimes they are hard to find.

Sometimes the ranchers are riding that country in December in two feet of snow still looking for a bull or two. Cattle can't winter in the mountains. If it goes much beyond the first snowfall or two, they will be dead. Cattle won't paw down to grass beneath the snow like a horse will.

But snow makes it easier to track them. After the first snow, the ranchers drive around in a four-wheel drive, usually with horses in a trailer in back, or drive around in a truck loaded with horses until they see cattle tracks. They usually get all their cattle before winter unless somebody steals or shoots one, and that happens every now and then.

The last day we all went down to the holding pens in Antelope Swale and gathered up the cattle, several hundred of them, and worked them all day. We had to get them in pairs and we had to sort the brands. We put them into a smaller lot then ran them through a squeeze chute into a series of pens with gates on the runway. A couple people on horseback held the cattle. The rest was foot work, usually done by the younger fellows.

The cattle came out of the chute two or three at a time. A rancher read the brands and said, "Don's gate," or "Bill's gate," or "Charlie's gate," or whatever gate that cow or calf or bull should go through. By the end of the day we had everything separated. Each rancher had his own cows and calves and bulls in one place.

We had a big to-do at camp that night. We fixed a big dinner in my trailer and in the line shack and had a party.

The next day everybody brought their own help and drove their own cattle home. I helped Glenn. Driving cattle home in the fall of the year is fairly easy. The cows want to get back to the home ranch. This is where they spend the winter and they know there's good feed. The old cows lead the way. Once they get started, they don't wander much. By this time the calves are three months older and a lot stronger. They weigh probably four to five hundred pounds. They aren't weaned yet so they are still with their mamas. When that old cow heads down the hill, they're all going. They string out real good.

That was Saturday night and I was three hundred and fifty miles away from home. I had to be at work on Monday. I bid Glenn and the others good-bye, turned Rusty around and rode back to Bluebucket Cow Camp. It seemed like I had been there only three days, I'd enjoyed it so much. I had wanted to be a cowboy all my life and now I was one, or something like that.

That fall I got well acquainted with all the fellows there. They treated me so well and made me feel like I was part of the bunch. They even asked my opinion on what to do a few times. That made me feel right at home and I am sure they meant it that way.

That night I got all ready to go, packed up everything, took down the roof to the "barn." All I had to do was load Rusty in the van, hook onto my trailer and take off down the road. I got up early the next morning and did just that.

On the way home I stopped at Sisters. I always stopped here to unload Rusty and let him walk around a little, stretch and relieve himself. I got home about six that night.

In all the years I hauled Rusty, and I hauled him all over the country, every time we came home, he would whinny when we turned onto Canyon Creek Road in Wilsonville. The horse van on my truck didn't have a front window, but it had a side ventilator that he could peek through. He always knew exactly where he was. Horses have an instinct that is uncanny.

Before I turned Rusty loose, I put him in his stall for about twenty minutes to get his circulation back to normal. Then I turned him out. He ran a circle around the pasture, stopped, shook himself hard, then lay down and rolled for probably five minutes. He did this every time I brought him home from a trip. He always found a dusty or muddy place to roll in.

In 1974 I went back for the Drewsey Co-op fall roundup. My good friend and neighbor, Bob Eastman, went with me. We had spent many hours together riding and around campfires, but this was Bob's first trip to the Drewsey area. Bob had his horse, Diamond. I had Rusty.

The cowboy staying at the line camp that year was a young fellow named Derrick Carpenter, who lived in the Drewsey area. His dad was a rancher in Drewsey.

When we pulled into Bluebucket Cow Camp, Derrick was out on horseback. We went on in and made camp. Bob had his trailer and I had mine so we each had our own place to sleep and eat. Having someone there with me made it much more fun and Bob was the best kind of company.

Derrick came riding in—a good looking, tall, slender, athletic cowboy who was an excellent horseman. He looked as if he could be part of a Zane Gray novel. He had a 44-magnum six-gun on his hip, which he carried every day wherever he rode.

He said he had been watching for us. The ranchers had told him we were coming. He was tickled to death to have someone up there. He had been there all summer, most of the time by himself. We struck up a good friendship with Derrick Carpenter right there.

His wages for June through September were twenty-five hundred dollars plus all that he wanted to eat. He would go to the store in Drewsey and charge his groceries to the Drewsey Co-op. He told us later, "You know, I can do this job all summer and I won't spend any money. I've got all my food and gasoline for my pickup. My truck is paid for. When I walk out of here October 1, I'll be twenty-five hundred to the good. How can you beat that?"

We had known Derrick was going to be at the line camp so Bob and I had brought fixings for some real nice meals. We both had good-sized freezers in our trailers. Bob was one of the best cooks I have ever known and I do pretty well myself. We had some tremendous meals and Derrick ate every meal with us: breakfast, lunch and dinner.

One day he said, "My work is caught up. There's some country on the far side of the allotment. Let's ride over there this morning and I'll take you on the most beautiful horseback ride you've ever been on. We'll go down into the headwaters of the Middle Fork of the Malheur River. There's not many people who get down there. We'll do some fishing.

He said, "It's kind of rough and we'll have to lead our horses down some of it where it's just too steep to ride and we'll have some logs to get over."

We saddled up and rode over to check the cows and gates in the area. We then rode on and up to the edge of a cliff. I could not see how in the world we were going to get down to that river. The river was so far down it looked like a piece of string.

Derrick Carpenter, rider for the Drewsey Co-op.

Bob Eastman and Don Carlton on the Middle Fork of the Malheur River.

We rode our horses on up another mile or so and got off. We started down. It was steep. If we had been climbing a hill that steep, I don't think we could have made it. We had some big rough places, some with downfall, but we got through them all. Derrick knew the way.

He was in such good physical shape I think he could have carried his horse down that hill. I was doing well just to stay on my feet. It took us an hour or better to get to the bottom. We came out to the Middle Fork of the Malheur River in country that not many people see.

There are no roads, just cattle trails. A few ranchers get in there and once in awhile a fisherman.

We rode down the river about ten miles to a not-so-steep trail that led up out of it. We caught several fish. We got back to camp about seven and that night we had big, beautiful trout for dinner. It was a long trip, but one of my most memorable trips. Just the isolation of this wild and beautiful place thrilled me.

Derrick had two cow dogs, Fooey and Satchmo. Fooey was half Pit Bull and half Border Collie. He was a big brute of a dog and one of the two best cattle dogs I saw in that Drewsey country. Fooey could grab a bull by the nose and hang on.

Most Hereford bulls are gentle, but they get obstinate if they get riled. They are no match for a dog; a dog is too quick for them. When a bull went on a rampage, old Fooey got right in and grabbed hold of the end of the bull's nose, the most tender part. He could almost throw a bull, hanging on and whipping him back and forth.

We were up there for nine days. It was pure pleasure. We had some big campfires, barbecued some good steaks and had a few drinks.

On the day Bob and I left Bluebucket Cow Camp for home, Derrick told us later, "I sat down on that porch and cried."

I knew just how he felt. He was up there alone all summer and all of a sudden along came a couple of people he liked. For a week he had real good comradeship and fun. Then all of a sudden, he was alone again.

Three or four years later Derrick built a home a little farther up the mountain from Guy Marshall's cabin. Derrick's two cousins helped him. Derrick was planning to get married and he and his wife were going to live there.

Bob Eastman and I went to Drewsey when Derrick was building the house and drove up to see it. You couldn't see the house from the road. By "road" I mean a one-lane dirt road with some shale rock on it and room enough for one pickup. Every now and then there is a place to pull over so vehicles can pass.

Derrick and his two cousins were putting hand-cut tamarack shakes on the roof. Derrick saw us, jumped off the roof, lit on his feet and came running over to us. He was tickled to death to have us there.

The house was made out of pine logs. Derrick had cut the trees and the shake blocks. An old timer down in Drewsey had come up and cut all the shakes for him. Other people around Drewsey who had specialties, such as wiring and plumbing, had helped him, too.

They had dug out a spring about fifty feet below the house, and had put in a thousand gallon tank above the house. A gasoline pump at the spring pumped water up to fill the big tank. The house had hot and cold running water.

Derrick was a genius with a hammer and nails and he had made a beautiful house. The inside was as nice as any home I ever saw. It had a big room with a fireplace in the middle. On one side of the fireplace was the kitchen. Patio doors led outside. It had two bedrooms.

Derrick got married and lived there for two or three years. Later someone from Boise bought it as a summer cabin.

After Derrick quit taking the summer job for the Drewsey Co-op, an old cowboy by the name of Millard Newell took the job. He and his wife, he called her Cookie, lived at Bluebucket Cow Camp for two or three summers.

Bob Eastman and I went over and rode with Millard during those years. Millard was an old timer who had been horseback all of his life. He knew all the tricks. He had a big white horse that must have weighed fifteen hundred pounds. That old mountain horse was solid. If Millard roped anything and hung on to him, that critter was as well as tied. That horse wouldn't fall down.

We were in camp one night with Millard after we had gotten in from our daily gather of cattle. We had a couple of cocktails and hadn't had dinner yet. Millard said, "Hey, there's an old black cow coming down there on the other side of the road."

We all looked. Millard said, "No, that's not a black cow; that's a bear."

Sure enough, a big old black bear was about two hundred yards away and across the road, the same kind of a one-lane dirt road as all the others up there.

We didn't see bears very often unless we surprised them. They usually stayed out of our way. As soon as this one heard our voices, he turned and disappeared, just vanished from sight. But he was almost a bear in camp.

The country above Drewsey is bear country. We'd see one occasionally when we were gathering cattle and ranchers were always reporting bear being around.

Byron Dunten stayed up at Bluebucket Cow Camp in the fall of 1986 to watch the cattle. He had a trailer, which he parked at the other end of the allotment 20 miles away. There was a little corral there and a pasture where he left some hay. When he'd wind up on that end, he'd put his horse in the corral and spend the night in that trailer.

On my way out of there in the fall of 1986, I stopped at the store in Burns and I ran into Byron.

He said, "I just got down out of the mountains. They got all the cattle out, but guess what happened to me."

I said, "What happened?"

He told me about his trailer being up there. He said, "I rode my horse in there one of the last days we were there. Half the windows were broken out. The door was busted open. The whole trailer was torn to pieces."

I said, "You mean a bear?"

He said, "That's exactly right. A bear came in there. I probably left some food out that had some odor to it, like bacon. That old bear was after food. He ate everything he could eat and tried to eat the canned food, but he couldn't get it open. He had everything torn to pieces."

That tells you something about a bear. When you're around where bears are, you can't leave anything lying around. They'll try to get in and get it, particularly stuff that smells strong, like bananas, ham and bacon.

Fall gather crew: Charles Dunten, Byron Dunten, Bob Eastman and Millard Newell.

17   Riding, roping and branding

During the time I had been going up to Bluebucket Cow Camp, I had become acquainted with another ranching family—Bill and Carol Robertson and their two sons, Rod and Rex. Bill and Carol lived on the main ranch in the Otis Valley. Rod lived about two miles down on the next ranch with his wife, Debbie, son, John, and daughter, Lisa. Rex lived about five miles on down on another ranch, with his wife, Rose, and their children, Billy, Darcy, Christy and Joe, who we called Joe-Joe.

The Robertson brand is the S Wrench brand, one of the most famous of the old western brands in Oregon, Idaho and Nevada.

One day when I was at Glenn Sitz's ranch, I was talking to Rod. They were going to gather heifers and take them to a pasture they were leasing at John Day. He asked me to go.

I saddled Rusty that next morning. It was freezing and Rusty was feeling so good he was walking on eggs. We headed down to the Robertson ranch. I thought, boy, when I go through the gate into this horse pasture and all these horses start running around, Rusty is going to get excited and I'm going to have my hands full. I sidepassed Rusty up to the gate, reached over and opened it. Just as I got the gate opened, Rod and the crew drove up. I closed the gate. They thought that was pretty good on a horse.

Rod said, "Hey, Don, why don't you round up those horses and take them back to the corral. Getting it done here would save us a little time."

I said, "Fine." But my heart jumped. With Rusty feeling so good, I thought if I started after those horses and they broke into a run, I was going to have a rodeo. I started after the horses. Sure enough, their heads came up and they watched me. They knew they were going to get rounded up. No sooner did I start for them than they broke toward the corrals. Every single one of them headed at a high run, bucking, jumping and just feeling good.

Rusty wanted to run. I let him out a little, but I had a short rein on him. The whole terrain was strange to me. I didn't know where it was soft or had holes. The horses ran a quarter mile to the corrals. I rode up to the gate and closed it. I was pretty proud that Rusty hadn't gotten rid of me.

That morning we rounded up two hundred yearling heifers. We loaded them into a stock truck and took them over to a pasture at John Day, across the mountains. They would hold those heifers there and sell them in the fall. By fall they would weigh about seven hundred pounds.

That day started a long friendship with the Robertsons.

Rod said, "Say, you ought to come up in the spring, about April. We're doing our branding then. We'll teach you how to rope a calf."

That sounded good to me. I was sixty years old then. I had always carried a rope and practiced on fence posts. I had learned how to keep a rope straight, coil it, clean it, but I had never roped anything alive.

The next April I was at the Robertson ranch. I asked Rod one night, "What's on deck for tomorrow, Rod?"

He said, "Tomorrow we're going to take six hundred head of yearling steers over to Wheeler Basin."

Wheeler Basin was in their BLM grazing allocation. It was on the desert rather than up in the mountains.

The next morning we got up around four and had a big breakfast. It was the first week in April. It can snow up there at that time of year. As a rule, it was down around twenty or twenty-five degrees in the morning, sometimes in the teens. We had dressed for warmth. We had leather chaps, heavy coats, wool scarves, gloves, rubber overshoes over cowboy boots and about anything else we could put on including long underwear and heavy socks.

We saddled the horses and left the ranch at six. We already had the six hundred head of steers sorted and in a field. All we had to do was open one gate and get them started for Wheeler Basin, which was around fourteen miles away. As we started out with those cattle, it started to snow. It got half an inch on the ground and quit. It was cloudy and cold and windy. There were five riders—Debbie and Rose, Rex and Rod and me.

Many times young steers and young heifers like these yearlings are hard to drive. They are frightened and spook easily.

Debbie Robertson and her horse, Elmer Fudd, and Rose Robertson loaded down with work clothes to ride in 28-degree weather.

We had to cross the highway about five miles east of Drewsey.

The yearlings went along well. We got them to the highway. Carol Robertson was there flagging traffic so we could get across. We got them across the highway and up into Wheeler Basin, which was about three or four miles from the highway. That was my first experience driving yearlings. They can be a real pain in the neck, but this morning they went along like little gentlemen.

But can they run! They are quick and they are fast. If one gets going the wrong way, it takes a good horse to catch him. You don't do anything quick with young cattle. You move slowly and let them line out or you can lose the whole bunch.

Bill and Carol brought a big stock trailer over and parked it on the Wheeler Basin side of the road, just inside a gate into the field we went into. They also left a huge thermos of coffee and a big lunch.

We came back down out of Wheeler Basin to that truck and trailer. It was cold. Rex grabbed that thermos. I could tell by the look on his face that he just couldn't wait to warm himself up with some of that hot coffee.

That kind of day makes the most vivid memories: the cold,

the snow, the steaming coffee. We did get cold, even with all the clothes we had on. Yet, it's a day I remember with great affection and satisfaction, a memory that I cherish.

One day Rod said we were going to a roping at Dick Edmundson's ranch. Dick was a neighbor to Rod in Otis Valley. They were going to start me on roping. This was a big thrill for me.

That morning we fed all the animals. At this time of year, we fed everything every morning. It didn't make any difference whether it was forty below zero or raining; we fed. There were cows and calves and bulls in all of the fields. The bulls were together, away from the cows.

Rod and Debbie, Rex and Rose and I drove over to a set of branding corrals about two or three miles on the east side of the ranch. We unloaded the horses.

Dick Edmundson, his wife, Pat, his father and mother, and a couple of other ropers were there. It's always the custom on a ranch that the head man or one of his family does the knife work: the castrating, ear marking and dewlapping. So the family is usually working the ground. The neighbors come in and do the roping.

Six hundred head of yearlings on the way to Wheeler Basin near Drewsey, Oregon.

The Robertsons back at the trailer after driving 600 head of yearling cattle 14 miles in 28-degree weather and spitting snow: Rose, Rex, Lisa, Rod and Debbie.

We were going to brand about one hundred twenty calves that day. When they brand cattle, a roper catches a calf by the head and starts him toward the fire. Another roper comes along and catches his hind feet and puts the calf up to the fire and stretches him out. The ground crew takes the rope off the calf's neck and puts it on the two front feet. The horses hold the calf stretched out in front of the fire.

They brand it, castrate it if it's a male, ear mark it, dewlap it, vaccinate it and dehorn it. When that little old calf gets up from there, he knows he's been someplace. It's no wonder they're hard to catch from then on for the rest of their lives.

Bill Robertson told me the first time I was up there, "Don, I know that looks cruel to you, but it's the only way we can mark these cattle where we'll know them."

I surprised myself. I did just about as well as most on the head catch. Heel catching was another matter. I don't think I have made more than six heel catches in my whole life, and I roped at the Robertson's for several years.

For one thing, I don't try it very often because I hate to waste

Rex Robertson seeks warmth in coffee after the bitterly cold trail drive.

Preparing for branding: Glenn Harris, Bill Robertson, Rod Robertson, Joe Cronin and Rex Robertson.

everyone's time. If somebody has a calf by the head and is waiting for someone to pick up the heels, if I start after it, the other fellows politely wait and I probably miss. That takes time, so I stick with the head catch.

One of the best things is for a roper to make a heel catch when throwing for a head catch. This happens when you make a good throw but your loop is a bit too big. The calf jumps through it. If you pull up that slack quick enough, you get his hind legs. You can drag a calf to the fire by his hind legs and you're not going to hurt him. You get him to the fire. Somebody else throws a rope in for his front feet and you stretch him out.

I learned some valuable tips that day. These were all young calves. I learned, number one, that if you don't have a clean head catch, say you have one leg in the catch, you forget it. Shake your loop loose and go after another calf. If you drag a calf with one leg pointing straight ahead of him and one leg down, it's easy to break the leg that's down. Unless you are expert at doing that and know when to let up and when not to, it's better to let the calf go.

The usual procedure is that one roper makes a head catch and another roper catches the heels. The person with the rope on the calf's head drags the calf to the fire. Once at the fire, one of the ground crew flanks the calf and throws him. The header gives slack on the rope just as soon as that ground crew gets his knees on the calf's shoulder or head.

The man on the ground takes the rope off the calf's head and puts it on the calf's front feet. The header backs up to tighten the rope again. This leaves the calf strung out there at the fire. It is incumbent upon the man with the heel catch to keep his rope tight enough so the loop won't slide off the hind legs, but not so tight that it hurts the calf. Stretching a calf too tight can strangle it.

I did not realize this and I might have been instrumental in injuring a calf that day. Rusty worked perfectly with the calves. When we got a calf up to the fire, Rusty swapped ends real quick and held the rope tight on the calf.

I let Rusty pull on the calf a little bit too hard. Later Rod told me, "Don, you want to be very careful when you've got that calf to the fire and somebody has his heels. The heeler is responsible for not putting too much tension on that calf, but once he gets to the fire, the heeler is also going to leave it to your good judgment how

Heating the branding irons in the fire.

Branding a calf caught by the head and heels.

tight you should have that rope. When you have the rope around
the calf's neck, you need it just tight enough to keep it from running
off or keep it from getting on its feet and getting out of the heel
rope."

All the ranchers that I worked with were very considerate of
a stranger's feelings in a crowd. They never said anything to
embarrass me.

It's always customary on the ranches on branding day to brand
all day long. The ranch doing the branding furnishes a big lunch
for the crew. That day Mr. and Mrs. Edmundson—Dick's mother
and dad—took a barbecue out there and cooked hamburgers for
everybody. They had potato salad and other things, too. We all
had a big lunch with ice cold beer and pop.

It seems as if the ranch wives try to outdo each other to see
who can fix the biggest, most wonderful noon dinner. I ate some of
the best meals in my life at the Robertson ranches or Tommy

Howard's or Edmundson's and the other ranches.

It took most of the day to get those one hundred twenty calves branded. After it was over, we had a cocktail party and munched on the leftovers from the big noon meal. The sociability and fun were tremendous.

I found that work around the ranch in the spring was more fun than any other time of the year. Everything is geared toward getting the herd ready to go to the mountains about June 1. When they go depends on the weather, of course, because it depends on how the grass is growing in the mountains.

Spring work means all the calves have to be branded and vaccinated and taken care of. Many of the cows have to be vaccinated; the bulls have to be vaccinated.

The best part is that we were working around the ranch house so we were not in the saddle all day. At noon we took our horses into the barn, tied them up to a manger full of hay and went into the house. We had a beautiful lunch or dinner, rested awhile and then were back hitting it again. We had more breaks. We were doing different things.

That first spring I got to where I could throw a fairly good loop on a head catch. I could not believe that here I was doing some of the things I had dreamed about doing all of my life. I was right in the middle of it, happy as a clam.

Bill Robertson and his good saddle horse, Private.

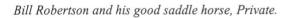

Why cowboys don't carry guns

In August the cattle have two more months to graze before they come out of the mountains. During this month the Robertsons move their cattle to a lower Forest Service allotment that hasn't been grazed, and close the upper allotment. I started helping them on the August cattle move.

We went up to the mountains and camped for a week. We gathered cattle from the far end of what they called the Rattlesnake Allotment and brought them down the mountains to the next allotment. This was a fun time. It wasn't as hard riding as it was in the spring when we drove cattle to the mountains.

Almost all of the land in the mountains belongs to the Forest Service except for a few privately owned plots. One of these plots is the ground that surrounds Alder Springs, about six miles above the Forest Reserve Line.

Alder Springs is a grassy meadow with aspen and pine trees, a beautiful camp spot. Alder Springs itself is piped out of the side of the hill and runs year around. It is fresh, ice cold mountain water and it is good.

John Adair went with me to the Robertson ranch in 1980. We took separate rigs so we had our own living quarters. John had a motorhome and pulled a horse trailer behind it. I had a horse van on my pickup and pulled my twenty-five-foot trailer behind it.

Johnny and I camped at Alder Springs. Debbie and Rod and Rex and Rose Robertson came up and stayed in their trailers. They put their horses in Ott Meadow. Ott Meadow is half a mile from Alder Springs and is fenced to serve as a horse pasture. We usually rode from Ott Meadow. Sometimes we hauled the horses out and somebody drove the truck and trailer back to Ott Meadow.

In August it can get pretty hot. But we were at six thousand feet in elevation so it didn't get stiflingly warm. The nights were cool and we wore coats. It made the campfire feel good.

About this time Jim and Lois Gardner, who were retired ranchers at Drewsey, started working for the Robertsons. They brought their travel trailer up and stayed, too.

Jim was an excellent cowboy and Lois was a good horsewoman. Both of them understood cattle and were good help to Rod. They also worked for many of the other ranchers in the Juntura–Drewsey area.

Many times cattlemen need extra help that they don't need the rest of the year, such as when they are moving cows. So Jim and Lois supplemented their retirement income doing this. They not only were good help, they were good company.

Jim Gardner was a small, wiry cowboy, and I mean cowboy. I don't think he weighed over one hundred forty pounds. He was very good with a lariat. He had a funny little backhand throw that he used when we doctored calves.

We would get a big bunch of cattle in a fence corner and maybe a dozen calves in the bunch had pinkeye or some other ailment. If someone rode through the herd swinging a big loop, it was pretty hard to get up on those calves. The loop swinging around spooked them. By now they were wary of the rope and got real smart about staying away from it. They hid behind the cows or anything they

Jim Gardner preparing for a cattle drive.

could. Jim would ride through that herd and, with his little hoolihan-type of throw, always come up with a calf. He took just one twirl to get his loop out, then threw it backhand. He was usually within ten or fifteen feet of a calf when he threw it and he was deadly with it.

Most of the days we rode quite a bit. We came in tired and ready for a highball. We hobbled the horses and put them out to graze. There was always grass up there. Of course their heads were down from the time they got out on the grass until we gathered them up for the night.

That first trip when Johnny came with me, we had a good week. That Saturday we were going to finish up our riding for cattle, so we made plans for a party.

Rod had to go back to the ranch. I told him, "Get hold of Glenn Sitz, your dad and mother, Pat and Dick Edmundson, and anybody else down there. Tell them to come up and we'll have a big smorgasbord and party Saturday night."

Glenn came up with his son, Jerry. Pat and Dick Edmundson were there. Of course the eight of us were already there: Rex and Rose, Rod and Debbie, Lois and Jim, and Johnny and me. Rod brought back some meat from their walk-in freezer down at the ranch. We fixed a big meal. Then we danced until two that morning.

I had my stereo in my trailer. Most of the dancing was right in my trailer. We let the table down and took out the chairs. That left about an eight-by-eight-foot area to dance in. At times the floor was completely full but we really had a ball.

The next August, Johnny came again and Larry and Pat Kelley came along for their first trip. By now Pat and Larry were experienced horse campers. They had been camping with us at Frank Riley Horse Camp, Quinn Meadows Horse Camp, Graham Corral, Sheep Springs, Squaw Creek and Three-Creek Meadow.

On the way we spent one night with Gale Struckmeyer at Hampton Station. Then we went on to Burns, turned north and went to Seneca. Seneca is just a filling station and store, which are both in the same building, and a few houses. It is cattle and hay country. From Seneca we turned straight east. We went through Logan Valley, which is one of God's most beautiful spots in the world, and on about thirty miles into Alder Springs.

Pat and Larry were delighted with Alder Springs. The first thing we did was have a drink of that good ice cold water. We made camp and hobbled the horses out in a grassy spot by Alder

Debbie and Rod Robertson.

Springs. Then Pat yelled, "There's a bear!"

We looked up and sure enough, just about thirty yards from where our horses were hobbled and eating grass was a pretty good-sized black bear. He looked at us. He evidently was headed down to the springs for a drink of water.

It isn't very often you sneak up on a bear. I guess he sneaked up on us. When he saw us, he turned around and ambled across the road. He wasn't in any hurry. He stopped a couple of times and looked back at us, then went on. He was going so slow that I had time to get my camera out of my trailer and snap two pictures of him.

The horses never did spook. That has been my experience so far as horses and bears are concerned. Several times in the wild I have been horseback very close to a bear, not on purpose, but we surprised each other. I have never had a horse throw a fit around a bear like you hear or read about. If a mountain lion is around where a horse gets wind of it, the horse spooks. But I have never seen one spook because a bear was close.

It was thrilling to see that bear in camp. We always saw lots of sign where bear had been in that country. Any old rotten log on the ground is always turned over where bears have been looking for ants or grubs.

Jim and Lois Gardner were riding with us again that year. Rod had the big stock trailer up there and Jim had a smaller truck. We could get about seven of the saddle horses in the stock trailer. We hauled the horses in different directions to get to the far end of the allotment, then spread out and gathered cattle. We brought them down into what they called Buttermilk Allotment.

We hauled the horses to Cat Creek. From there we rode up into the Rattlesnake Allotment, which was the farthest one north. It was one big mountainous allotment and one big ride. It was also rough country, some covered with pine trees, some with juniper and sagebrush. There was grass everywhere. The North Fork of the Malheur River bordered Rattlesnake Allotment on the northeast.

We rode up on Rattlesnake, then went southeast to a place where we could get down to the North Fork of the Malheur River. We could get to the river at only two places—one at each end of the allotment.

We rode to the bottom end to get to the river, then rode the river and gathered what cattle were in there, brought them out the other end and back up the hill.

It was so steep going down into the river that we led our horses down the hill. This is the only place I think I ever saw Rod Robertson get off a horse and lead him. In some places there were downed trees that we climbed over and the horses jumped over— straight down hill. It was tough.

I was the oldest guy and it was hard on me. Jim wasn't with us on this trip; he had gone horseback around the other way. I was over sixty-five at that time and that jaunt down that hill took just about all I had to offer. Every step I took, I went down a foot or two in elevation. It was jarring.

When we got down to the river, it was certainly worth the trip. We were right on the North Fork where very few people ever get. I wished I had brought some fishing tackle.

We rode up the river, riding in the river probably half the way because the mountainside was so steep. It was a real gorge.

We picked up about twelve or fifteen pair of cattle. When we got to the other end in more open country, we picked up another fifteen to twenty pair. We started back up the hill toward Anderson Springs, which is at the top of the hill on Rattlesnake Allotment. There is a holding pasture at Anderson Springs of about five hundred acres. The spring is in that holding lot.

By the time we got down that hill, rode the river, gathered the cattle and drove them back on top, it was getting late in the afternoon. It was also getting hot. The cattle were going slow and they were hard to move. We had to take it real easy with them. There were several dug-out reservoirs for water holes along the way. We stopped at each one and let the cows rest a bit, then pushed them on. When cattle get tired, they are hard to move. They try to dodge out. The calves hide. It was work all the time.

By the time we got to Anderson Springs and got the bunch in the holding lot, it was around six in the afternoon. We were all tired. But it was the kind of a day that you work at and you are kind of pleased with yourself at what you got done.

Riding that country horseback is the only way we could have done that job. No one can ever do what we did that day on a motorcycle or a helicopter. It simply has to be done horseback. The country is too rough.

Two or three days later we had gathered everything except about twenty pair. Rod always counted the cattle. He knew how many he had in the allotment and how many should come out. To count them, he waited until we drove them through a gate. Two people who were used to counting got on the other side of the gate and counted the cows and the bulls, not the calves.

Rod brought a couple of mechanical counters along. The person counting the cattle just clicked the counter each time a cow or bull went through the gate. This way the person didn't have to remember where he was in counting, which is hard when you have three or four hundred head to count.

It was getting on toward the end of the week. Debbie, Lois, Pat, Larry and Johnny were going to drive the cattle up close to Crane Prairie. Rod, Jim and I were going back to Rattlesnake to look for the strays that we had missed. Rod drew me a little map and gave me an area to ride. He showed me where I should come out with the cattle and where I should meet him and Jim. By this time I was fairly well acquainted with the area.

We rode out of Cat Creek. I went around the mountain part of Rattlesnake Allotment and came in on the other side to a big canyon where Crane Creek starts. I rode down the canyon to pick up anything I could find. I got hold of five pair in that big canyon. It was probably five miles long.

When I came out at the bottom, I was taking them up toward Anderson Spring. I was having a bit of a hard time. The day was hot and some of them did not want to go. It had been hot for quite a few days and the dust in some places was four or five inches deep. About the time I was getting to the top end of the canyon, I could hear thunder and see lightning south of me.

My yellow slicker was tied on my saddle. The thunder was getting louder. The lightning would flash then the thunder would clap. The flashes and the claps got closer together. Pretty soon there was lightning and right after it, thunder. I knew the storm was getting close.

I got out into the open and saw black clouds coming toward me. I was headed straight south; the storm was headed straight north and was within a mile of me. I thought, before that gets here I'm going to put on my raincoat, which I did. I also had a plastic cover for my straw hat, which I put on. About the time I got all that done and buttoned up, it started to rain.

It was the first time I had been caught out in a heavy lightning and thunderstorm. I was right in the middle of it. It was a bad hummer.

Inside of five minutes, four inches of dust was four inches of mud. The raindrops came down in a gully washer. Well, here I was. I had always heard that in a thunderstorm I should get off my horse and get away from the trees. I didn't know what to do. I didn't want to get off and tie my horse because he was spooked a little bit. I knew he felt better with me close to him, talking to him. That always has a quieting effect on a horse.

I had read not to get under trees, to get out in an open space. I hated to get out in the middle with that storm coming. I said, "To hell with it. I'm going to go right up under that great big pine tree." It was a double pine tree growing out of the same stump, about one hundred eighty feet tall. I backed my horse, Blackie, right up under that tree and we sat it out right there.

I was scared by this time. It sounded like the lightning was hitting everywhere. I could hear it crackling. It was raining hard and the wind was blowing. It had cooled all of a sudden from a hot day to a rainy cold day and the thunderstorm came with it. I sat there for about half an hour until it blew over.

Pretty soon the clouds were gone and again we had a nice day with the sun coming down. It felt good. I had gotten a little chilled. I didn't get wet, but I didn't have a warm coat with me. In the next ten minutes, the sun came out real strong.

I lost my cows just about the time the rain started. The lightning crackling all over spooked them. They all went in different directions.

I was not too darn sure exactly where I was, but I was pretty sure. I thought I'd just look around and see if I could find any of those cows. About that time I heard a "whoop, whoop, whoop." It was Jim chasing cows.

I yelled at him and he hollered back. Pretty soon here came Jim and the cows crashing through the brush. We wound up with twelve or fourteen pair and got them back to Anderson Springs.

Jim had had the same experience through that storm. He said, "Where did the storm catch you?"

I told him. He asked what I did. I told him.

He said, "You know, Don, I did the same thing you did. I just didn't want to get off that horse and I didn't want to get away from the shelter of the trees."

I said, "I was praying most of the time."

He said, "I was, too."

We had several little squalls of rain during that trip. There is one thing about the Northwest, if you are in the mountains in August, you will more than likely see thunderstorms. It is very seldom you run into one as bad as we hit that day, though. I have never seen one that bad before or since and I have been in several.

It started twenty-one forest fires that day. The rain put out a lot of those. Several of them burned until the Forest Service got to them and put them out. The heavy rain helped keep the fires from spreading.

Larry and Pat hit it off with Rod and Debbie and Rex and Rose. Rod and Debbie invited them back the next year or anytime they wanted to come up and help with the cattle. We made plans right then to be back the next year. They wouldn't make it, though, because Larry had heart surgery.

In August 1983, Pat and Larry Kelley and Johnny Adair and I went back to Drewsey. We had our own rigs: my trailer, Johnny's motorhome, and Kelley's camper. We lived very comfortably, which helps when you're out working hard. When I was young, I didn't mind a tent, but now I like that nice bed in my trailer, a shower in the morning and the indoor bathroom.

When we got there, Rod said we were going to camp over on Cat Creek. He said, "Alder Springs is a much better camping place, but most of our work is going to be close to Cat Creek. It'll save a lot of time and a lot of moving if we camp over there."

So we went to Cat Creek and set up camp. Cat Creek didn't have the nice spring water that Alder Springs did, but there was horse water in the creek with a nice little meadow there. A three hundred-acre horse pasture adjoined Cat Creek where Rod and Jim kept their horses.

We knew if we turned our horses into that big horse pasture with theirs, it would take them the week we were there to establish the pecking order. The horses would be skinned up. There was the chance that a very dominant horse in the group would run one of the others through the barbed wire fence.

So we made a picket line in the trees behind our camp for our horses. We also hobbled them in the meadow after we got back in the evenings. We brought them in at dark to the picket line and threw them their hay. They usually just picked at it because they were full of good grass.

We had quite a bit of rain in 1983 when we were at Cat Creek. I have a trailer awning that extends about eight feet. We set up everything underneath that awning and ate our meals beneath it. Every night we built a big campfire.

Debbie and Rod fixed up a canvas stall in the trees for a shower. They had water bags that were dark and had little pads in them that magnified the sun's heat rays. Each one held ten gallons. Debbie left them out all day on top of the pickup. Even on a cloudy day the water got quite warm. On a sunshiny day, it got hot.

On top of the shower stall they had a place to hang the water bag. Each one of the bags had a half-inch tube and a shower head that came down from it. Right at the shower head it had a little valve to turn the water on and off. When we came back from riding, everyone was able to clean up.

It was during this trip, that I decided to quit riding horses due to my back troubles. My pain became apparent to the others as well. Rod kept an eye on me. About the time I would get the cinch undone, Rod just happened to be next to me. He would grab the saddle, take it into the truck, and throw it over the rack. That fall I sold my horse, Czech Cowboy, to Pat Kelley.

The next spring I was talking to Rod. He said the Forest

Service had given them a new allotment. "It's one allotment above Rattlesnake Ridge," he said. "It's across the North Fork of the Malheur River. Remember the old cabin and the old barn we could see from Rattlesnake Ridge across the river, over on Flag Prairie? That's it. We've got all of the Flag Allotment.

"We'll put the cattle in the Flag Prairie unit first then move them out in August to the Mountain unit. So when we go up in August, we'll pull around over there. It's quite a bit further," he said. "There's an old barn over there and some old corrals and an old bunkhouse. There's a little cabin, which has been used as a cook shack. It's a newer building. It was a Forest Service building that someone hooked a Caterpillar up to and dragged in there. It has a cooking range that uses bottled gas. There's a big tank of gas outside. We'll cook and eat in there. We'll bring our trailers up to sleep in."

He said, "Debbie's dad, Bob Christensen, Jim and Lois, you folks and John and Lisa will be there, so we'll have a pretty good crew riding that country."

That sounded good to me. After selling my horse, I couldn't go completely without something to do. So I bought a Honda 110 trail bike. I drove it into my horse van and took it up to Flag Prairie. I enjoyed the Honda. The ranchers use them on their ranches now and would have a hard time ranching without them. One thing about a Honda, though, it won't jump a creek or jump a log. You can't get through rough country with it. But on flat lands and out in the meadows, you can do a whole lot with a Honda. So I was able to help, even without a horse.

Pat and Larry took their horses, Cowboy and Bo. We had to camp a little bit away from where the other folks were because we couldn't get our rigs into that area. We made a nice camp by another corral and a big pasture. Pat and Larry put one horse at a time in the pasture. With one horse in the corral and one in the pasture, it was easy to catch the one in the pasture.

Pat and Larry had a Golden retriever, Ellie. She was a big, beautiful dog, a nice dog. They always took this dog on our trips, but they had the good sense to leave her in their camper when we went out for cattle. She knew nothing about cattle and could have fouled things up on a cattle drive.

Ellie loved those mountains. When we weren't after cattle, she would go along. Any dog covers about five miles every time a horseman covers one because the dog is all over the country. It's amazing the amount of ground they can cover.

That year we had a big time. So much of the fun is in the companionship. In the mornings before we set out, we would have big breakfasts. Every night we would have a cocktail hour then a big dinner. We had some excellent cooks in camp and we all took our turns, including me.

On this trip we were gathering pairs and Larry came busting out of the brush with one cow and two calves. He was trying to get around them and he was at a dead run. He was sweating and he was mad. You can get awful mad at an old cow who doesn't want to go where you want her to go.

Debbie saw him so she rode after him. She said, "Larry, Larry, which one of those calves belongs to that cow?"

Larry was upset and he said, "Hell, I don't know."

She said, "You're fired!"

Everybody got to laughing so hard I think both the calves and the cow got away.

Larry Kelley and Jim Gardner enjoying life after a hard day gathering cattle. (Photo by Patricia Kelley)

Around the campfire at Flag Prairie: John, Rod and Debbie Robertson and Debbie's dad, Bob Christensen.

Moving cattle gets to be real work, but there are fun situations. This was just the third year that Larry had done any real cattle work and he was really after that old cow.

The North Fork of the Malheur River wasn't too far from the cabin at Flag Prairie. The water was around forty degrees. If you wanted to, you could go swimming or put your feet in it, but you'd freeze in a minute. It was good fishing.

I mentioned earlier that trained cattle dogs are indispensable when gathering cattle or driving cattle. On flat and level ground, you don't have much problem with the cattle. But when you get up in the mountains and get into tough country, and some of it is straight up and down, or get into mahogany thickets, you need a dog.

Mahogany is a small tree that branches out and is thorny and thick. Sometimes you can't get into mahogany even on your hands and knees. An old cow or calf can go through those thickets like a dose of salts. A dog in a place like that is irreplaceable.

Lodgepole pine thickets are also tough to go through but a cow can get through any of them. A cow is a hardy, tough, rough animal. She can go places that a man can't go. And after those old range cows have been up in that country, they are not afraid of anything. When some of them head for those thickets, they are trying to lose that cowboy. You sure get mad at them.

One year I was having trouble with one special cow that kept turning back. I told Rod that when the year was over I wished he would butcher that cow and send me a pound of the hamburger because I would enjoy eating it.

He said, "Don, that's why cowboys don't carry guns. There would be a lot of dead cows and a lot of dead dogs."

The Robertsons had a unique situation with their land. Their leased land and their deeded land ran consecutively back into the mountains to the far end of all their allotments. I think it was about forty miles back into the hills.

In the fall of the year, they opened the gates. The old wise cows knew it was about time to get back to the ranch and get some hay. They wouldn't leave the green grass, though, until the weather started turning a little bad. But when a little snow flew, some of those old cows headed for the ranch.

Every day the Robertsons went out and gathered the cattle that had drifted into the big meadow near the ranch. They brought them in, sorted them and put them in another field. That way they kept count of exactly how many came in each day.

At the end of September they went looking for those that hadn't gotten out of the allotments. There were always a few pairs and some bulls that hadn't come in.

One November I was up at Rod and Debbie Robertson's ranch. It was during elk season. All the cattle had been taken out of the mountains except for six bulls.

There was snow on the ground. Rod and I put two horses in the stock trailer. I had brought my saddle but not my horse. I was riding one of the ranch horses, Private, a good honest horse. Rod took his favorite horse, Hummer. We headed for the mountains north of the ranch in a four-wheel drive pickup pulling the stock trailer. As we climbed to about five thousand feet elevation, we were into a foot or more of snow in some places.

On our way up the mountain, we pulled into Alder Springs where a group of ranchers had a hunting camp. Rod's son, John, who was about fourteen years old, was there. Most the other people were adults. They had a small twelve-foot Oasis trailer. John was asleep in the trailer when we drove in. He woke up, got up and went to pick up his boots. They were frozen to the floor. His boots had been wet when he went in and there was no heat. They had to take a hammer and knock them loose.

We went on to Buttermilk Allotment, which covered about six thousand acres. We drove around until we found tracks of the bulls. One set of tracks looked like they were headed down toward Alder Springs. We headed down that way and saw the bulls standing in a little clearing.

We were probably six miles from the Forest Reserve Line where there was a big corral and loading chute where we could load the bulls into the stock trailer. We unloaded my horse, Private. It was rough country with downed trees.

Rod told me, "Whatever you do, don't try to hurry those bulls along. They'll go at their own pace. Don't try to push them. One of them," and he pointed out which one, "is real hard to get along with. Just follow him along. Keep him pointed toward Reserve Line and put him in the big corral there."

Rod said he'd work around and find another pair and then

Rod Robertson and his good cow horse, Hummer.

he'd drive the truck and stock trailer half way back to the Reserve Line on the road, a very narrow mountain road.

He said, "I'll park the trailer there. If you get down to the Reserve Line first, you come back and pick up the truck and trailer. If I get down there first, I'll do the same thing. I'll see you at the Reserve Line."

By this time it was about noon on a cold winter day. It was probably twenty degrees.

It was as Rod said. Hereford bulls are not normally mean to handle, but they can get real ringy if you try to push them. I stayed probably fifty feet behind them. They ambled along. Bulls certainly don't cover ground like a race horse. They tried to turn off. I pulled out and went to the side to keep them going straight.

Every once in awhile the bulls stopped. I stopped when they did. If they didn't start again pretty quick, I touched Private with the spurs. He'd go towards them at a slow walk. They'd start on again.

The closer I got to the Reserve line, the darker it got. It was close to four o'clock when I passed the truck and stock trailer that Rod had parked on the road. I went on about a mile past the stock trailer. It was getting dark and I didn't want to ride back up that road in the dark. I had those bulls going pretty much the right way. It was clear, not many big trees or obstacles. So I trotted Private back to the truck and trailer and put him in the trailer. I got in the truck and drove the truck and trailer a little ways past where I had left my bulls and stopped. The truck and trailer were now parked about a mile and a half from the Reserve Line.

The bulls were still in the area I had left them. I unloaded Private and rode back around the bulls and started them again toward the Reserve Line. I got my bulls down to the Reserve Line and drove them through the corral gate and closed it.

By now it was getting dark. I trotted back to where I had seen two other bulls and got them about half way to the Reserve Line. About this time a pickup came up behind me. I was really glad to see it.

A fellow got out and came over and said, "I bet you're Don Carlton."

I said, "You're sure right."

He said, "Don't you know me?"

It was Bob Christensen, Debbie Robertson's dad. Bob and I had known each other a long time. Bob's dad had been in the milk business in Portland, and I was working at Mayflower Farms managing dairy product sales.

I asked Bob if he and his wife would go back and get our rig and drive it down. I had to get those other two bulls down to the Reserve Line.

They went back and got the truck and trailer and got back to the Reserve Line about the time I did. I was proud of myself, getting those four bulls. About that time Rod showed up with the other two bulls so we got all six bulls in that trip.

We wanted to get the bulls back to the ranch. Rod had a big bale of hay in the trailer. We threw that bale of hay into a big pen across the road. We put the horses in there with the hay and closed the gate. We went back over and loaded the bulls into the stock trailer, which made a full load, believe me. We got all the bulls back to the ranch that night and went back for the horses the next morning.

When the cattle come out of the mountains, they come down to the home ranch. In the fall, there is still pasture because it has been growing since they took the hay out of the field in August or September.

The cattle stay in the pastures until they eat the pastures down. While they are eating, they are also fertilizing the pastures. Manure, of course, is about as good a fertilizer as you can get. Once the pasture is gone, the cattle go on hay.

Ranchers usually have to feed hay to cattle for six or seven months out of the year beginning sometime in November. They can't afford to buy the hay they need so they put up their own. Robertsons had about ten different fields at the ranch. They irrigated these meadows and grew between two thousand and three thousand tons of hay a year.

In that country they don't get much rain, maybe six or eight inches a year. So most ranchers stack the hay outside then cover the top with loose hay. They still lose a lot of hay to the weather.

The Robertsons built two big hay sheds since I have been going up there. They bought all the parts—lumber, cement, everything—and built it themselves. Even on a do-it-yourself basis, the first shed cost over $10,000. But they saved so much hay that they built a second shed. Now they have two huge hay sheds that they fill with baled hay; then they stack more outside.

The Robertsons feed about fifteen tons of hay every morning

from sometime in November until about June 1. It takes two people, one to drive the tractor or pickup that is pulling the big trailer and the other to feed.

The trailer is twenty-feet long and eight feet wide. They pull the tractor into the hay shed and load it with the baled hay. They feed maybe thirty-five bales in one pasture, depending on how many cattle are out there, then ten bales down in a corner pasture, then fifteen bales in another pasture and so on. For a guy like me, who buys hay three or four tons at a time, the amount of hay they use each day is astounding.

When I'm there I help by driving the tractor or pickup. Rod does the heavy work, of course. We drive out in one of the fields. The cows see us coming and they head toward us. As I drive slowly, Rod cuts the strings off the hay bales and kicks the hay off the truck.

We make a long string of hay on the ground, maybe half a mile long, so all the cows can get up to it. If we kicked the hay off in one place, the strongest cattle would get everything to eat and the calves wouldn't get anything.

I have never been up there in the real deep winter time, but I know it has gotten as cold as forty degrees below zero. The cattle don't seem to have any trouble with the cold so long as they are getting good grass hay. But they have to be fed every day.

For a hundred years hay was baled with wire. Imagine opening three hundred bales of hay every day and the wire from three hundred bales of hay. Pretty soon you'd have a mountain of baling wire that would be hard to do anything with.

A lot of times when the wire was cut, a piece broke off and got in the hay. Sometimes a cow would eat it. The ranchers put a magnet in the bottom of a cow's stomach to attract the wire and pull it all to one place. But a lot of cows have died from wire in their stomach.

Wire was a real problem on ranches for years. Then the steel shortage came along about ten or fifteen years ago and a real strong nylon twine was developed to bale hay with. There isn't a rancher in this country, I would venture to say, who would even think about going back to wire bales. They can burn the nylon or throw it in the garbage pit. They don't have to worry about the cows eating metal pieces. One man can pick up all the twine discarded in a day.

The nylon twine was developed out of necessity. No one in all those years had thought of it even though we had had nylon ropes for years. There are still many things that are going to be thought of today, tomorrow and the next day. Someone is going to make a million dollars out of what we take for granted, just as we did wire-baled hay and limped along for a hundred years.

I have never seen a skinny animal on the Robertson ranch, including dogs, horses and cows. Every animal is well taken care of. This is just the way they operate.

Bill Robertson is happiest when he's looking out in that field and he sees his cattle sleek and fat and they are about ready to go up in the mountains. They have spent a good winter; the calves are healthy, bright and shiny and growing.

One time I got up there in the spring and I asked Rod how they were coming out on hay. Usually it's nip and tuck those last few weeks before the grass greens up and they head for the mountains.

Rod said, "Oh, pretty good. We had a little left over. Dad's still trying to stuff all that down the cattle before we take them to the mountains."

I said, "How much?"

He said, "Oh, about one hundred tons."

But that's the way Bill Robertson is. He is not satisfied with a hungry animal on that place. He wants them fat and rolling. Of course, the bigger the cow, the more money it brings.

Getting into the mountains on time is very important for these ranchers. They are feeding fifteen or more tons of hay a day. If they were buying that hay, it would probably cost at least seventy dollars a ton. At fifteen tons a day they are not going to waste time getting to the mountains. If they can get into the mountains on June 1, nobody waits until June 2 or June 3.

By the same token, when they are coming out of the mountains in the fall, they don't start bringing the cattle out fifteen days early. They don't bring them out two hours early. They wait until their time is completely up, and then bring them out of the mountains.

Most of the hay is native German timothy hay. The pasture is lush with this beautiful grass. I would take my horse out and hobble him in a corner of the pasture. With all that grass he would be plumb full in an hour. The pasture was too big to turn him loose. It would have taken me a month to catch him with all that feed, and in a pasture like that he would have gotten so fat that he could just hardly waddle.

That is a problem on a ranch. They don't have the time or patience to keep a horse up, turn him into a pasture and take him out a couple of times a day. Consequently, many of the horses gain too much weight. Horses are like people, some get fatter than others. The ranchers have to take some of these horses out of the pasture and put them in a corral and feed them hay for awhile to slim them down.

20 *Cow caesareans and other odd jobs*

The ranchers use two-wheel trail bikes to do a lot of their work. The Robertsons have four or five. Of course, the kids love to ride the bikes. Most would rather be out on their Hondas than on their horses.

Before the days of motorbikes and motorcycles, the ranchers kept a wrangle horse in the corral, which they would saddle and go out and run in the horses with. Now, they simply crank up the Honda.

At five or six in the morning, when that Honda starts up, you see the horses in the pasture down around the creek and willows stick their necks straight up. They watch the rider; it's usually Bill Robertson. If he starts toward them, when he gets to one certain place, about three hundred yards away, they all line out and head straight for the corrals at a dead run. Their tails are up. The sun is just coming up. They buck and kick on the way. They are feeling good. It is a beautiful sight.

One man can work a lot of cows on a Honda. When the cows come down from the mountains in the fall, they drift in toward the Robertson ranch and gather out in a big field at the end of the road. A cattle guard prevents them from coming further into the ranch. They go to the waterhole in the pasture and graze around there.

So every morning in the fall, Bill Robertson goes out on his Honda to the pasture and starts the cattle down toward the house. He goes all the way around the back edges of the pasture, gathers up all the cattle and puts them in the big pastures and hay fields east of the house. He used to use a saddle a horse to round them up. Now he does the work on his Honda.

That does not mean a Honda is going to replace a horse. When the cattle are up in the mountains, in that rough country, they just don't make anything with an engine on it that can take steep hills or rocks and deadfall.

This country has millions of rocks. One piece of ground on BLM land, where both Glenn Sitz and the Robertsons have cows, is named Rocky Basin. Believe me, it was not misnamed. It is so full of rocks that you cannot ride a horse through there without stepping on rocks every foot. Horses hate it. Even those that are raised on the ranch detest those rocks. They look at the rocks and almost look back at you as if to say, "Hey, dad, what are you going to do? You expect me to walk on this stuff?"

There are some places where a horse can put his feet where he is not on a rock. But in a lot of places, he cannot miss the rocks. An unshod horse would not last too long.

Horses raised in this country have extremely good, tough feet. The rocks seem to stimulate growth of a bigger foot and most of the horses raised here have bigger feet than horses in other places.

One of the things we humans have done to horses—the papered, well-bred horses—is to create a small-footed horse. Judges in most horse shows, especially in the past thirty years or so, have preferred the small-footed horse. That's fine in a sawdust arena, where the horse isn't ridden all day and is not worked.

But, give me a horse with good solid big feet any day. Big feet build a strong foundation, just like a strong foundation under a tall building. A dainty-footed horse has a hard time in the mountains. I like to see a horse wear at least a size one American shoe and a size two is not too big on a big horse.

Most good Thoroughbreds have good feet, as do Arabs. An Arab is a smaller horse as a rule but they do have feet that better match their size than the Quarter horse does.

Quarter horses are my favorite except for their small feet. I think the show judges are responsible for that. I have had Quarter horses that were extremely good horses but I had to be very careful because of their small feet, especially in the kind of riding that I did.

Speaking of Rocky Basin reminds me of a story about Glenn Sitz. We were going to Rocky Basin one fall to gather as many cattle as we could find and bring them in. I was with Rod Robertson and we met Glenn on the road. Rod and Glenn talked about it and decided we would all go together and bring all the cattle out. Then we would cut out the different brands when we got them home. That conversation was two or three days ahead of time.

It got to be the day before we were supposed to go to Rocky

Basin. I asked Rod if we were going to meet Glenn. He said, "Let's run up there tonight and talk to him." So we did.

They talked. Glenn was great for saying, "Well, I don't know. Well, maybe. Well, I don't know."

He and Rod talked for half an hour and I was lost as to what was going on. Rod and I left Glenn's place and headed back to Rod's ranch in the pickup. I said, "Rod, I got lost in that conversation back there. What did you and Glenn decide to do?"

Rod said, "Damned if I know. We'll just go on up there and if Glen's there, we'll go ahead. If not, we'll gather what we can and bring them on down."

Glenn Sitz was a hard worker, a fine rancher and a lot of fun. Everybody liked Glenn and I had many good times with him. But it was very hard to pin Glenn down. I would hate to be an IRS man questioning Glenn. Glenn would drive him straight up the wall.

A lot of the work done on a ranch is on foot. Often the ranchers want to separate a bunch of cattle, for example, in the fall they want to separate the calves that they are going to wean. They bring fifty or sixty head of cattle into a large corral. The cattle are all mixed up, with bawling cows and calves.

The large corral feeds into a smaller corral that feeds into the alleys of the main set of working corrals. One of the ranchers lets out two or three cattle at a time, which run down the alley. Three of us are on gates. Maybe I'm on a gate where all the heifers are going and someone else is on a gate where all the steers are going and another one where all the cows are going. The person working the cattle yells, "Steers!"

Whoever is on the steer gate opens that gate. It opens out into the runway so it acts like a funnel. The steers run in through the opening.

Say the next one comes along and it's a heifer. They go in the heifer gate, and so on. This might go on all day long.

There isn't too much sleep around the ranch for a night or two. Every mama is looking for her calf and every calf is looking for a mama. They are all trying to get to where they last nursed.

I have done the footwork in cold weather, in the rain and mud where the feet get a bit heavy, and on a real hot day when I was about to burn up.

The ranchers use the corrals to separate cattle for vaccinating, for treating to control mites or lice or other parasites, and for other reasons. If they have to doctor a grown cow or bull, they use a squeeze chute to immobilize the animal and hold it so they can do what they need to do.

On the other hand, if they are in the mountains and have to doctor a cow, it takes two people who know a whole lot about what they are doing. That cow has to be headed and heeled and stretched out on the ground. Two people have to hold her. Or, if the rancher has a good roping horse with the rope tied fast to the saddle horn, the man can get off that horse to doctor the cow. The horse is trained to keep the rope tight.

Several things can affect a cow in the mountains. She could have pink eye. She could have an injury. She could have hoof rot. It can be any one of many ailments. The cowboy and rancher has to be about half veterinarian.

Everyone on the ranch is busy. They all assume part of the responsibility. When there is a job to do, they all pitch in and get it done.

When I first started going on the Robertson Ranch cattle drives, Carol Robertson, who is Bill's wife and Rod's mother, would be on most of the drives, and Debbie and Rose Robertson on all of them. The ranchers' wives, aside from fixing meals that are tremendous, seem to find time to get the dishes done, do the washing and the other housework, and still do the big drives where they need riders. They are out there on horseback, sometimes for ten or twelve hours a day.

Everyone on the ranch has things they specialize in. Debbie works hand in hand with Rod. She does almost as much riding as Rod does. On the days when they are riding, and sometimes it's seven, eight or nine days in a row, she simply adds the riding work to her chores of getting all the meals, keeping the house going, and so forth. She keeps up with all the medications on the ranch, and keeps them handy so when they need them at a moment's notice they know where to get them. Debbie also helps Rod in the vet work.

The Robertsons often hold their calves over for a year before selling them. They separate them, keeping the steers separate from the young heifer calves. They pick out one hundred fifty or so of their best heifers.

The next year the heifers replace some of the brood cows. The first year they calve, they are separated and driven down to Rod's ranch. They are put in a field close to the house and fed hay.

Rod and Debbie stand a twenty-four-hour watch at calving time. From January through March, one of them is up and keeping tabs on the heifers. A good percentage of these heifers would die in giving birth to a calf if somebody wasn't there to pull the calf.

Rod and Debbie have had so much experience and have watched first-year heifers for so many years that they know when a cow is a few hours away from having a calf, just by the way the heifer acts. The heifer's tail is kinked out to one side and she might be walking the fence.

I watched this marvelous feat. A heifer was walking the fence and pretty soon there was the calf's feet sticking out of her vagina. The heifer didn't have that calf right away, so Rod ran her into the nursery set up in the barn, and into one of the two birthing stalls. The heifer put her head through the stanchion. The stanchion clicked shut, which controlled her head. She couldn't do anything but stay in the stanchion.

Rod got a stainless steel chain, put it on those two legs that were sticking out of the cow and started pulling.

I marveled at the birth of this little calf, weighing fifty to sixty pounds, as it hit the ground. Rod went over to the calf, put his finger in the calf's ear and wiggled it a little bit. The calf's eyes blinked and in just a few minutes he was standing, looking around at this great new world that someone had just dropped him into.

Rod is a good cow doctor. In ninety-nine out of one hundred times, Rod pulls the calf and it comes right on out. But every now and then one of these first-calf heifers' calves is placed wrong. As a rule the calf comes out head first with the head and neck lying right along the front legs. The front legs come out, then the head, then the body of the calf.

Sometimes the head gets turned backwards, where it's looking over its shoulder. In those cases Rod puts a big plastic sleeve on his arm, puts lubricant on it, and inserts his hand into the heifer's vagina and straightens out the calf. Most times he can work the head around to where the calf can be born and come out fine.

When he can't straighten the calf out, there's a problem. This is when most people would call the vet. But when you are fifty miles away from the veterinarian's office, what do you do? Well, Rod has learned to do caesarean operations.

I watched Rod do a caesarean operation on a big cow. The cow weighed about eleven hundred pounds and simply could not have her calf. The calf was twisted inside. I helped Rod drive the cow into the nursery barn and get her head in the stanchion. We got a rope on her hind legs and tightened the rope up to a stout post kitty-corner across the big stall. The stall was probably twenty-feet square. The cow was stretched out.

Debbie went into the house and got all the tools that they needed, the anesthetic and so forth. Rod deadened the area and evidently the cow felt absolutely no pain. He clipped the hair off the area right down to the skin. Then he scrubbed it well with alcohol. Next he made an incision in the skin about a foot long, and then cut into the womb, reached in and pulled the calf out.

The calf came out completely normal, lying on the ground for a minute blinking his eyes. Obviously he was going to be all right.

Then Rod put the cow back together. He took suturing material and a special suturing needle and sutured the womb. He disinfected it, gave the cow shots of penicillin and sulfa, then sutured the outside skin back together. He had two complete sewing jobs. He got it all back together and washed it clean.

The cow got up pretty quick after the anesthetic wore off. The cow and calf both lived and both did very well. I have seen Rod do this several times since that first experience.

Not every rancher can do this. No one ever told Rod Robertson that some things couldn't be done. That is the way he approaches every problem. Rod is a an extremely good rancher, a hard worker and an excellent cow man.

One time we came in and here was a cow with her uterus completely hanging out. It was about two feet long and eighteen inches wide and looked like a pocket that was turned inside out.

I said, "My God, Rod, what do we do now?"

He said, "Well, we've got to get that back in there."

Debbie, of course, is always right there with all of the material, whatever is needed. She headed for the house and came back with the doctor bag, the disinfectant and so forth.

We ran the cow into one of the nursery stalls and got her head in the stanchion. Debbie brought out a clean piece of plastic sheet. She and Rod held up the uterus and washed it off with chlorinated water. The uterus had manure on it, sawdust and dirt. They washed that completely clean with medical soapy water. Then Rod put his big long, one-time, single-service glove on his hand and arm and up to and over his shoulder. He got that womb and shoved it back into the cow. The womb tried to come out again so he had to suture up the vagina, which had been torn on this cow. He sutured that up to where the womb would stay in.

I have seen Rod do that several times since and I have never seen him lose a cow. He said he has, but I don't think he has lost very many. This is something most ranchers would call the vet for. But it's a one hundred mile round trip from Burns to Rod's place.

Rod also does his own pregnancy testing (preg testing) on his herd. To do this they use a cattle chute. They run all the cows they are going to preg test that day into a large corral. Then they run about eight or ten cows into a smaller corral on one end of the larger corral. Out of the end of that small corral is a chute that only one cow can go down. They get the cows lined up in that chute, which holds eight or ten cows. At the end is a squeeze chute. The cow goes in, puts her head in the stanchion and it closes on her neck so she can't move. Then they pull the lever and tighten the sides of that chute so the cow is caught.

Rod puts his long glove over his hand and arm and up to his shoulder. He lubricates that and goes into the cow's rectum. He can tell if the cow is pregnant and about what size the calf is. If she isn't pregnant, the cow is separated into another pen and goes to market. The ranchers' crop is calves and a cow that doesn't have a calf is long gone.

The Robertsons have a band of ten or twelve mares, or did have. They are getting away from that a little bit. The mares run in the hills with a stallion.

Rose Robertson is an excellent rider and breaks the new colts every year. The ones that turn out real good they keep. The others they sell. Almost all the saddle stock on this ranch are geldings. This follows my old rule of thumb that a good gelding is very hard to beat as a saddle horse.

One place that really bears this out is when they leave the horses on the mountain when they are going to be working cattle. They turn them into one of the horse pastures up there rather than hauling them back and forth to the ranch. A bunch of geldings get along much better if no mares are with them. A mare is going to run a bunch of geldings and that sometimes causes problems.

I just don't think you can beat a good gelding for a good saddle horse. I know I am going to wear this phrase out, but it bears repeating.

There is a lot of machinery on a ranch of this size. The

machinery is where Rex Robertson is head man. Rex understands machinery so well. He has a big shop and does most of the repair work on all of their equipment—tractors, mowers, pickups, everything.

When ranch kids are not in school, they are on a horse, working along with everybody else. They learn from almost the day they hit the ground the responsibilities of running a ranch. When I first started going to Drewsey, Rod and Debbie Robertson's kids were five and eight years old.

John Robertson, nicknamed Dubs, was driving a tractor by the time he was eight. Lisa Robertson was helping with the housework and the cattle. I can still see Dubs driving the pickup down the road when I could hardly see his head through the windshield. He was driving the pickup back and forth between the ranches when he was probably ten years old. A lot of times he was doing a man's work on a horse.

The kids drag the pastures to break up the manure and scatter it evenly. The cows are in those fields in the fall and are dropping manure all the time. That manure doesn't do much good in little cow pies. So when the cows are taken out of the fields and headed to the mountains, the first job that's done is to drag those fields with big drags behind a tractor.

It takes a lot of time because there are many acres. It's a boring job. But the kids get paid for it, so they are eager to do it. They do a good job, too; dad is watching.

When the kids work in the hay fields or babysit, they are paid for it. All of the kids have a bank account and their own money. They learn how to spend it and how important it is. Instead of trying to run them down to have them work, they are interested in working.

All the neighbors in the Drewsey area help each other. Of course, no one ever runs out of work on his own ranch, but if somebody has a big job such as driving a lot of cattle, branding or other task, there is always whatever help is needed.

In 1978 I was headed to Drewsey for the fall work. I had Blackie, my horse, with me. I had gotten a late start and got to Hampton about four in the afternoon. Hampton is about halfway between Bend and Burns and a little over halfway between my home in Wilsonville and Drewsey.

Hampton was just a wide spot in the road. It had a filling station and restaurant. There was a house behind and part way up the hill where the foreman of the Hampton Grazing Co-op lived with his wife.

The Hampton Grazing Co-op was owned by twenty-three ranchers, all of them living within one hundred miles of the area. The ranchers trucked cattle or young stock into the Hampton Grazing Co-op and left them there from June to October. This was the high desert and although it looked barren, it had a lot of feed.

These ranchers had hired a foreman to run and operate the grazing co-op. This was a big job. They usually had about two thousand head of stock on the co-op, most of them yearlings. The yearlings would come off the co-op in the fall and go to feedlots.

The co-op had two or three big working corrals and probably forty smaller corrals where they could separate cattle for brand, sex, size and so forth. The corrals were just off the road at Hampton and they had water.

When I pulled in, I had my eye on one of the smaller corrals where I could put Blackie. I thought, by gosh, I'm going to go up and talk to these people and see if I can spend the night.

I went to the house and knocked. A woman came to the door. I introduced myself and told her what I wanted, that I was hauling a horse and headed over to another ranch.

She was very nice. She told me that her husband was out working cattle, but he would be home soon. She told me to go on down to the corrals and make myself at home.

So I did that. I put Blackie in one of the small corrals. The water tub in that corral was turned upside down and I wasn't too sure about the water. So I thought I would wait for the rancher. Pretty soon here came a couple of guys in a stock truck. I watched as they unloaded their saddle horses.

Gale Struckmeyer was warm and friendly. He said, "I sure appreciate you stopping at the house and asking to put up your horse. We have people who come through here with horses, stop and make themselves at home and don't say a word. Half the time they leave a big mess for us to clean up."

He wanted to know if I needed any hay. I told him I had plenty of hay, that I had all my feed with me.

He said, "Well, is it a broken bale?"

I said, "No."

He said, "There's no need to break a bale of hay and then have to haul that mess. I'll bring you down hay. Here, let's fix up this water."

We turned over the tub and he showed me where the water was and how to get it turned on. Here again, one of the things that helped me get acquainted was my horse. He was a good looking horse and to another horseman, that opened doors. Gale really admired Blackie.

Gale was small and wiry and looked like a cowboy. He had western clothes, of course, a cowboy hat, gloves, very worn chaps, boots, spurs and a 44-magnum on his hip. The reason for the 44 was that he never knew what he was going to run into on the desert. It wasn't so much for protection but for an animal that has broken a leg and needs to be put out of its misery. The 44-magnum was part of Gale's dress every day.

Gale and I got off to a great start. He asked me to come up to the house and have a beer or a drink with him, which I was glad to do. He introduced me to his wife, B.J. She was very friendly. It was the beginning of a solid friendship.

Gale wanted to know where I was going and I told him.

He said, "We've got plenty of riding around here if that's what you're looking for. You won't have to drive that far."

I said, "I'll take you up on that one of these times."

He wanted to know when I was coming back. I told him in a couple of weeks.

He said, "You know, about that time we have fifteen hundred head of yearling steers up in those hills north of Hampton here.

Gale Struckmeyer, foreman of Hampton Grazing Ranch. (Photo by Patricia Kelley)

We have to bring those steers down out of the hills and move them about five miles down the road. A lot of the ranchers will be here, but I'm going to need all the riders I can get."

He said, "If you'll come back about then, I could use your help." He gave me a date when they were going to move the cattle.

I told him I would be back.

I stopped on my way back from Drewsey. I got there a couple of days before the drive started. This gave me time to get better acquainted with Gale and B.J. I had bought some steaks and groceries in Burns on the way back. I fixed dinner for them that night in my trailer.

We rode around the place and did some work from the pickup. He had to check out the water each day. One of the biggest jobs on the co-op was to keep water to the stock. There were several wells around and lines that led to a series of tanks from each well. The tanks had to be where the cattle could spread out to graze, yet not be too far from water. Many times the lines had leaks.

In several places they had diesel engines that were operated by floats on the huge watering tanks. When the water level in a tank dropped, the engines would automatically start up and pump water into the tank. The floats and engines had to be checked to make sure they were operating. It was quite a job maintaining that water system.

We also moved a few head of cattle around.

Gale gave me a sketch of the co-op and a map. The Hampton grazing acres bordered the ZX and Viewpoint acres, which were miles and miles to the south of us. It covered one awful lot of ground.

Eighty-thousand acres is a lot of land and two thousand animals are a lot of cattle. If you figure it out, that's forty acres to an animal. The grass isn't growing out there like a lawn, but there is a lot of feed. Of course, some years are better than others depending on the spring rains. This desert was new to me. I was familiar with the Drewsey area, which was on the edge of the desert and bordered the pine forests of the higher country.

There is an old story about the desert land and how the feed grows. That is that in some of those areas a cow has to learn how to graze at a high trot to get enough to eat because she has to cover a lot of ground.

Hampton itself is about four thousand feet in elevation and the hills behind it go up another thousand to two thousand feet. This is truly desert with sagebrush and juniper trees, but it also has grass. I was surprised at the amount of feed these 80,000 acres produced.

When you drive along on the highway and look out across that desert, it looks flat like a table top. Well, that's deceiving. If you ride across the land horseback, you can't see very far except for the high points. You can be riding along and suddenly you come upon a little lake or a dry lake. You can't see it from a long way off. There are so many gullies, little hills, rises and depressions that you just don't see very far.

This desert has lots of antelope and coyotes. We saw both of them every day.

The big day of the gather came. I got up about three-thirty that morning. The first thing I did was go out and throw Blackie his hay and grain. I came back in and fixed my own breakfast and got ready. I saddled up early.

Gale told me, "We'll load up the horses and haul them back into those hills to the far end of the area that those fifteen hundred steers are in. Then we'll spread out and gather the steers. I'll show you the general direction we have to bring them."

The country isn't wide open; a lot of it is cross-fenced. So we had to go where the gates were.

I met several of the ranchers. Darrel McCall and Lowell

Foreman were both young cowboys who were real horsemen. They knew what they were doing. Gale very thoughtfully put me with them. There were other sons or ranchers who were in the co-op as well.

Right away they looked at my horse. Blackie was well put together. He was jet black with a little brown in his flanks, brown in the muzzle and a big white diamond on his forehead. He was a King Ranch-bred horse, a registered Quarter horse. My gear was good and my horse looked good. They liked Blackie. I instantly made friends with these two people.

They had a big stock trailer. I loaded Blackie in with their horses and we took off.

There were twenty-two riders on this trip; several were guest riders.

It took several trucks and big stock trailers to haul those twenty-two horses back into the mountains. We unloaded. Gale, the foreman, gave everybody territories to ride. Lowell and Darrel and I went to the far corner of the allotment where the pasture covered about five thousand acres.

As we rode back, they pointed out the area to me. We were up in the hills behind Hampton. Even though we were about five or seven miles back, we were uphill and could see the whole country down below. We could even see the highway. It was beautiful country, all sagebrush, sparse grass and juniper trees.

Darrel and Lowell gave me a canyon to ride. I was to pick up everything in that canyon and start them going down hill, which sounded like a big job. It really wasn't. There were probably forty or fifty head in this canyon.

I went up to the far end and started riding across it and every one of those cattle started down hill. If we had been driving them uphill, it probably would have been a much different story. One man couldn't have done it.

I came out of the bottom of that canyon and Darrel and Lowell pointed out the route we were going to take. As I got down there, I could see other yearling cattle moving way ahead of us. These were all white-faced Herefords or Black Baldies, which are a cross between an Angus and a Hereford. It made me almost dizzy to look at them. It looked like the ocean, like waves, like the whole ground was moving.

This was the beginning of the biggest cattle drive I had ever been on. We gathered fifteen hundred head of yearling steers with twenty-two riders. The cattle all had to go through one gate.

When you're driving cattle, you like to get cattle strung out so they are not in a bunch half a mile wide. The cattle drive and move better when they string out. They follow the leaders. There are always some in the drag—the slow ones, the ones that want to turn back, that don't want to leave. But most of them move along pretty well.

We were on a dirt, two-rut road. When that entire fifteen hundred head got strung out coming down the mountain, they made a string between a mile and a mile and a half long.

Gale was on a big yellow palomino horse he called Yeller. They were having real trouble with one black steer. This hummer was really wild. He didn't want to go and kept breaking back. This had been going on for about half an hour. He was bound and determined he was going to stay.

The steer broke back through two cowboys. Gale shook out his rope. He figured he would have to rope him, tie him to a tree and come back and get him. Gale started after that steer and the steer started to run. It takes a good horse to catch an active yearling steer.

Gale was after that steer wide open, fast as he could go, standing up in his stirrups. He had his reins and his slack rope in his left hand and was swinging his lariat with his right hand. He was just ready to turn loose the loop to throw at the steer, when Yeller stepped in a badger hole. Gale did a double somersault, hit the ground and was knocked out.

So here we were, way up in the mountains. They had to get him down and into the hospital in Bend. He was pretty badly hurt and spent about six days in the hospital and all winter and part of the next summer recuperating. He had broken several ribs and his left collar bone.

Luckily the horse did not break his leg. He was gimpy for a few days, but straightened out and was OK.

This is one of the reasons these ranchers don't like badgers. You can't catch badgers and tell them not to dig holes, so the ranchers destroy them. It's just one of those things that has to be done.

The rest of us finished the drive. It was a thrilling sight to look down and see a mile or more of cattle ahead of us.

I had had nose surgery about a month before and I had told my doctor where I was headed and what I was going to do. He had told me to stay out of the dust.

He said, "Be as careful as you can. It could cause you some trouble."

Well, the main work was right there in that back end—in the drag—and it's the toughest work. All of the others up in front are moving along pretty well but those in the drag are tired or want to go back. Riding in that back end was bad. This was dry sandy country and the dust was flying.

It seemed like most of the guest riders on this ride wanted to ride up alongside the string to keep the cattle from straying. There were three or four young women, twenty or twenty-five years old, who were having a big time. They were toward the rear end of the string but they were riding way out from the dust. They would gallop up toward the front and then they would gallop back. They were within thirty or forty feet of the cows.

When they galloped back, they really messed things up. The minute they would turn their horses around the cows would hesitate. These people were out having a big heyday and a nice horseback ride. They did not even know what was going on back there in the drag and did not realize how much trouble they were causing.

I heard Darrel and a couple of others in the drag grumble. They were upset. Yet nobody said a word to the riders causing the problem.

It seems almost to be a code with people on the ranches not to say anything. I think it would have been better if somebody had said, "Hey, look, I know you don't realize this, but you should move along slow with the cattle, always in the direction they're going unless you have to go back to push a stray back into the bunch. Don't ride upstream to them or close to them, because that's the opposite of where we want them to go."

Gale had told me before the drive, "You know, Don, I've got some folks up here who I would just as soon not be here. They are here to ride the horses and they don't understand much about driving cattle."

I couldn't leave Darrel and Lowell because there weren't too many riding the drag, so I stayed in the drag during the whole trip. I have seen cowboys with bandannas over their noses and I found out why they do that. Even with staying away from the heaviest part of the dust, I could not have handled it without that bandanna over my nose.

Darrel McCall was in that dust and was literally covered with it. It was tough, hard work. I tried to get on the leeward side where it wasn't that bad.

When we got back, I apologized to Darrel for not helping more in the drag. I told him about my nose. I didn't want him to think I was dogging it, laying out there to the side. But there was no way I could have handled the thickest dust with my newly-operated-on nose.

He said, "My gosh, you shouldn't have been back there at all."

I think folks killed three rattlesnakes on that drive. With that many animals moving, they stirred up whatever was out there to be stirred up.

We got the steers down out of the hills. The sheriff of Deschutes County, the county that we were in, was also riding with us. He liked horses and he liked that kind of country. He had the highway blocked when we got there. When you cross the highway with a mile-long string of steers, you don't do it in five minutes.

It took about an hour from the time the first steer broke out on the highway until the last steer was on the other side. We actually had to go about a mile down the highway and then across to the other side. It held up traffic and the dust along the highway was terrible.

After we got the cattle across the highway and down to the pasture, we had a big lunch that B.J. and some of the others had put up.

That evening, Lowell and Darrel and I had dinner at B.J.'s.

I left for home the next morning but stopped in Bend to see Gale. I pulled into the hospital parking lot with my horse in my truck and my trailer behind me. I went into the hospital.

They had operated on Gale's shoulder the day before. He was in bed all taped up. His arm was in a sling sticking out and braced up.

He said, "Say, I heard you had some riders on there that weren't too good."

I said, "In my book, they didn't help us. They were pushing the steers back toward us about half the time."

He said, "Well, they won't be on that trip again, I guarantee you."

Later, when this was all over, some of the fellows talked to Gale about the riders. Gale called the ranchers whose guests these people were and asked the ranchers to please never ask these people back on the drive again.

I wish I had known some of the things I know now when I first started going to the ranches to help. It would have helped me tremendously. Most ranchers enjoy the help from another person on a horse, unless they act like these riders did. They like the company.

My advice to anyone going to a ranch for the first time is don't jump in. The ranchers don't like their cows to be run around the country. They move them slowly and let them take their own gait, especially if they have a long way to go. Once cattle are hot and overheated, they are going to turn back or try to break. If you get them upset and you have a whole bunch of them, it's very possible to lose the whole bunch. They will break right back through you.

If you are in a long string of cattle and driving them, like we were doing with this bunch of steers, don't ever gallop back toward the back end unless you get one hundred yards or more away from the bunch. By going the wrong way, you are confusing the cattle.

If you are going to help, ride along the sides and go slowly. Cows are going to walk slower than a horse does so you have to hold up and wait for them. At that point, don't turn around and gallop back so you can ride further.

From that time on, I always left early for Drewsey so I could stop at Hampton and ride with Gale.

After that first year at Hampton in 1978, I rode every year with Gale Struckmeyer. On Memorial weekend in 1982, Pat and Larry Kelley and I made a special trip to Hampton Grazing Co-op. I was going on over to Drewsey. Pat and Larry didn't have that much vacation so they were going to Hampton then back home.

We left Wilsonville on May 27 in pouring rain. As we went over Santiam Pass, in the Mount Jefferson–Three Fingered Jack area, it was spitting rain and snow. It cleared up as we came down the east side, and the highway was dry from there on. A few clouds drifted in the sky.

We stopped only for lunch and arrived in Hampton about four in the afternoon. Gale and B.J. and Harold Latrell welcomed us warmly. Gale had cleaned the pens, troughs and alleyways for us.

We parked our rigs in the big round corral next to the smaller corrals where we put our horses. All the cattle were out in the grazing areas so we had the corrals to ourselves. The corral fences helped break the desert wind, which is particularly pervasive in the spring. We set up camp.

Kelleys had their Golden retriever, Ellie, a beautiful purebred nice dog. Gale and B.J. had a female blue heeler, who was good company for Ellie.

The weather was chilly and our heavy coats felt good. The horses were feeling good and were real snorty. Blackie was a fairly calm horse but he was in strange country. A horse is more likely to buck when he's in strange country, especially if it's cold. The weather is a little different; the terrain is different; the smells are different. A horse has a very keen sense of smell and hearing.

I did not want to saddle up the next morning in about thirty-five or forty degree weather with that wind blowing and have a rodeo on my hands. At this point I was sixty-seven years old. Twenty years ago it wouldn't have bothered me much. But the older I got, the more careful I got.

I always tried to ride after I got into a strange place. Being hauled all day is work for a horse. He is standing up fighting the motion of the ride, so he is tired by the time he gets to where he is going. I took advantage of this. I would saddle him up and take him for a short ride. It let him see his surroundings and get a bit of the starch out of his soul. It helped settle him for the next morning's ride.

I told Larry, "I'm going to go for a ride and take some of the ginger out of old Blackie."

Larry had a big bay Quarter horse by the name of Lucky. Pat had her little palomino Quarter horse, Dusty. Larry and Pat and I saddled up and rode across the desert. Boy! Was I glad we did. Those horses were gentle and well trained but they were also well bred and well fed. They had a lot of life to them. All we would have had to do was kick them out and we would have had a ride. All of them would have bucked sky high.

They were walking like they were on their tippy toes. All horsemen know what I'm talking about. When horses are that tense, the saddle lifts up a little bit. If no one is on the horse, you can see a little space between the back end of the saddle and the horse's back. You can feel that tenseness when you are in the saddle, too. They stayed that way for about half an hour.

We rode straight out into the desert and far enough to get the tension out of them. Then we cantered a bit, rode around and brought them back to camp. By the time we got back to the corrals, they had settled down. They knew a little bit about where they were and felt easier about it.

After our ride, B.J., Gale, Harold and Harold's two daughters came down for a visit. Harold was working for Gale. Harold was divorced but had his two daughters now and then. He was young, tough and confident. If anything he was too wild, but he was a cowboy. As far as he was concerned, there wasn't anything he couldn't do horseback. He had no thought of having an accident. He took some real chances, almost scary sometimes. But he was a good cowboy and could ride most anything.

We sat around telling stories. South of Hampton out in the desert is Benjamin Lake. At times, when there are heavy snows, it forms a fairly decent lake. Most of the time it's just a watering hole for cattle.

Gale told us, "You know, a guy just pulled in here with a boat and California plates. He wanted to know where Benjamin Lake was. I drew him a map and showed him how to get there," he said. "He didn't ask me if there was any water in it and I didn't volunteer the information."

Harold had worked for a rancher in Montana and was over there in the wintertime. There was an old fellow who lived in a small cabin on a small ranch. He lived a rugged life. He had a sick horse that he put in the back of his pickup and took to the vet. The vet told him there was no way to save the horse and he would just have to do away with him.

The old fellow said, "Well, I just as well shoot him then. I hate to. He's been a good horse."

So he shot him right there in his truck.

Harold said the weather was below freezing for about three months. So this old guy left the dead horse in the back end of his truck for ballast.

This sounds pretty raw to a lot of people. But I can see that happening.

The next day Gale and Harold had to do some water work. They said we had just as well take some rides because what they were doing wasn't much fun and we couldn't help. They had a leaking water line back at one of the wells.

We saddled up our horses and headed for Thompson Meadows. The horses were still feeling good and I was glad we had ridden them the night before. It had frozen during the night. The water buckets had ice on the top.

We went up to a spot in the hills north of Hampton. These hills were like the desert, with sagebrush and juniper trees, only pushed up another thousand feet. We could ride in any direction.

There was an old homestead up there and some old working corrals. This was grazing land that the Hampton Co-op used. This was old, old time ranching country with old homesteaders' cabins, little one-room affairs, ten or twenty feet square. Some didn't even have windows.

Clouds came up and spit a little rain and snow at us. We were dressed in long underwear, chaps, heavy coats and slickers.

That night we all went up to Gale and B.J.'s house and ate turkey dinner.

We had a campfire at the corral that evening. There is something about a campfire that brings out the best in everybody. You look into those flames and somehow your talk is always

At Thompson Meadows above Hampton, Oregon. (Photo by Patricia Kelley)

subdued, as if you would infringe on somebody if you talked too loud. It's a special feeling when you are sitting with good friends around the campfire.

The next morning we were to move a bunch of cows out of one of the far pastures. When I say pasture on this co-op, I am talking five hundred or a thousand acres. The only thing that would be any less than that would be the horse pasture of about five hundred acres and the working corrals. The horse pasture isn't that big because there aren't many horses.

We were going to haul our horses about ten miles out into the grazing land to a spot called Brown's Well. This was an old cabin that had been there for years. The Co-op built a concrete block house around the well. On this well they had a diesel engine and a huge water tank. The engine pumped water out of the well into a reservoir on a small hill above the well. The reservoir had pipes down to several water tanks for watering cattle. When the reservoir got low, a float on it automatically triggered the diesel engine.

Water is essential on this desert. If there is no water, it doesn't make any difference how much feed there is. You can't use it. You can't put the cows on it because the cows have to have water.

On the drive in, we came across a black cow. She was big. She looked like a black Angus. She didn't belong in the pasture she was in and needed to be trapped and loaded into the truck.

Gale had ramps and some rails that he carried on the side of the truck. With these, he could load the average cow, even if he had to rope her and pull her up with a horse.

Gale stopped. He was going to run this cow back into another pasture to load her. My horse was the last one in the truck, so we jumped Blackie out of the truck. Harold chased the cow on Blackie, but he couldn't get her. She was as wild as a deer and would not go back to the fence. She started on a long run down the road. Harold followed her at a gallop for about two or three miles.

Blackie was blowing pretty hard so Harold stopped to change horses. We dropped the ramp on the truck, got out Harold's horse and loaded Blackie back in. Harold rode after the cow on his own horse. He still couldn't catch her. When he got close to her, she would charge him. A mean cow like that is dangerous.

Harold said, "There are some big juniper trees over there. I'll get her over there and rope and tie her to a tree."

I thought to myself, gee, he sure shouldn't do that alone. If he trips, that old cow will kill him.

Gale told him, "Harold, whatever you do, stay back. Get that old cow in a corner but wait until we get there. Don't do anything."

Homesteader's cabin at Thompson Meadows. (Photo by Patricia Kelley)

We were getting close to Brown's Well so we went on to Brown's Well and unloaded the horses. Gale and I went looking for Harold. Pat and Larry waited at Brown's Well.

We found Harold. Harold had roped that cow, had jumped down off his horse and was running around the juniper tree. That old cow was after him. He ran around and around the juniper tree, keeping the tree between him and that mad cow. She would have killed him if she could have gotten to him.

The cow finally got tangled. Harold took a half-hitch in his rope on the tree and finally got out of there. But there he was in chaps, heavy clothes and spurs, running away from a cow around that tree. He was young and strong and wasn't afraid of anything.

The old cow had evidently been in loco weed and was crazy. Gale and Harold were going to load her up and take her back to the corrals. They backed up the truck as close to the cow as they could. They dropped the tailgate on the truck, then dropped the steel portable railings into brackets on the side of the ramp. This made the ramp a walkway with rails on each side.

They were going to try to goose that cow up the ramp, which they had done many times with other cattle. That's why they carried those ramps and rails with them. It's easier to load an old cow into a truck and drive her back twenty miles than it is to drive her back with a horse, especially a cow as goofy as this one was.

They put another rope on the cow's neck and tied it to the front end of the truck. I was to man the rope.

Gale got on his horse. They got the rope from around the tree and put another rope on the cow and tried to pull her into the truck using the rope on the cow going over the truck and tied to the horse. But they just couldn't do it.

Harold was on his feet in back of the cow, trying to drive her up the ramp. Normally that would work. But this cow was completely nuts. She got halfway up the ramp, then she snorted and went straight up in the air. She got one leg under one of those side railings and pulled the railing completely out. The railing came down pinning Harold under it on the ground.

I thought the cow had stomped him. I would not have given ten cents for his life at that minute. But the cow hadn't touched him and he scrambled out from under the railing.

We still had ropes on the cow, one rope going to the horse, and the other one tied securely to the truck so we could kind of control the cow. The cow was fighting the ropes. She jumped straight up again, went over, lit on her back with a big grunt and never opened her eyes. She was dead.

Gale dropped on his knees on the chest of the cow to see if he could start her breathing. He could not revive the cow. She was flat dead.

The cow was crazy and could have killed somebody. If Harold had been out there alone, I think he still would have roped that cow and tried to do something with her.

We left the cow where she was and went back to Brown's Well. We got Pat and Larry, took our lunches and headed out from Brown's Well.

Brown's Well is a picturesque old place. Bill Brown is part of Oregon's history. Supposedly he owned more horses than any other man ever had in Oregon, about three thousand head. They roamed on the free range in that part of the Oregon desert. Brown's Well was part of his old homestead. It was a thrill to be there and ride out of a place like that. A good bit of Oregon history had been written right here.

We went out to Stud Horse Pasture at the far end of the grazing co-op pastures. There were some Viewpoint Ranch cows in there. Viewpoint is now part of the great old ZX Ranch, one of the largest ranches in Oregon, maybe in the Northwest with thousands of acres.

We gathered about eighteen Viewpoint pairs that had gotten through the fence. Gale had found out about these cattle from one of the grazing co-op members, Jim Easley. He had an airplane and had flown from his own ranch, which is in Powell Butte about a hundred miles away, to Hampton. He had seen these cows from the air and figured they were Viewpoint cows and had told Gale.

We drove the cows back into the Viewpoint pastures then rode the fence to find the break. We repaired it and rode back to Brown's Well.

It was a beautiful, nice ride. It was cold and we had on many clothes. Somehow the adverse weather makes you remember those times with great fondness, at least for me. I remember that whole day so well and how much we enjoyed it.

B.J. was waiting for us at Brown's Well when we got back about four in the afternoon. We headed back to Hampton just in front of some dark clouds. The desert can be dangerous for someone who doesn't know it. If you are out there in a pickup truck and it rains, you will get stuck in that sand and mud just so quick you

Looking down on Brown's Well homestead. (Photo by Patricia Kelley)

won't know what happened. So we were running ahead of the rain.

We were there four days and four nights. Pat and Larry were leaving Monday morning. Sunday night we got in early and had a cocktail hour in the corral. We built a big fire. We had smoked salmon and fresh King crab for snacks.

Pat Kelley's brothers and father were King crab fishermen. They owned King crab boats that worked out of Kodiak, Alaska. They lived at Depoe Bay and Newport, Oregon. They brought the boats down at least once a year to Newport for repairs.

Pat and Larry didn't hurt for crab meat. I had many good crab and halibut and salmon feeds at their house. Her brothers, Ted and Gary Painter, had been home and had brought a bunch of King crab. So Larry and Pat brought several pounds of King crab with them. We all have freezers in our rigs and we had the freezers full of frozen King crab.

On Sunday night we set up a couple of folding camp tables and cracked the crab. We also thawed out top sirloin steaks. We cut those sirloins up in small strips a little over an inch and a quarter wide and an inch and a quarter thick and barbecued them.

I can remember Gale, with his mouth full of King crab, saying, "You know, I never in this world thought that we would be out here in the middle of this corral, eating King crab and smoked salmon and top sirloin steaks."

Gale and B.J. proved to be good friends. They came to the Willamette Valley in the summer of 1983. We had a big party for them on Canyon Creek Road where they met all of our other friends.

Gale looked like a cowboy. If you met him in a steam bath with nothing on, you would have been able to tell he was a cowboy. He was well built without an ounce of fat on his body.

One day in October of 1983, we got a phone call that Gale had died of a heart attack. He was just fifty years old. He had gotten up from bed during the night, B.J. told us later. His chest was hurting, so he took some baking soda thinking the problem might be gas. He died right there on the bathroom floor.

B.J. and Gale were about sixty-six miles from Bend and about that far from Burns so they were far from a doctor. Jim France, who was the sheriff of Deschutes County, where Bend is, was a close friend of Gale's. B.J. called Jim right away. He took care of sending the ambulance, the medics and so forth. But it was too late.

Here was B.J. all by herself. She tried to give Gale mouth-to-mouth resuscitation for an hour, trying to bring him back.

Eating King crab in the desert at Hampton: B.J. Struckmeyer, Don Carlton, Gale Struckmeyer, Larry Kelley, Harold Latrell and Harold's two daughters. (Photo by Patricia Kelley)

I have seen some good trainers and I have seen some who get by simply because the person who brings the horse to them is a novice. The trainer acts mysteriously and tries to impress the person. Some of these trainers think they know what they are doing, but I would say there is one good trainer out of five. I think I am being generous there.

Of the good ones, though, Wil and Beverly Howe are two of the best. I first met Wil and Beverly at one of the Hermiston, Oregon, B'nanza Horse Sales. B'nanza has three sales a year— spring, fall and winter— and there are always seven to nine hundred horses that sell in each sale. Wil and Beverly would show up and have a horse or two in the sale. I was interested in them because they always came with good horses.

They would buy horses they liked, train them and bring them back. Wherever they went to horse sales, from Red Bluff, California, to the Northwest, they almost always had the high-selling horse.

One time at a Billingsley Horse Sale in Madras, they came in with two good looking sorrel geldings. It was a two-day sale and I was camped at the sale yard. They unloaded the two geldings, saddled them up and rode them around. Of course, they drew a crowd. Those horses looked good and they showed well.

Wil reached over and slipped the bridle off the horse he was riding and put the reins under the horse's neck. The horse behaved as if he had the bit in his mouth. They topped the sale with those two horses.

Wil is a tall, lanky cowboy. You would know he was a cowboy if you saw him a mile away. He wears his long cowboy boots up over his pant legs. He has had a full beard since I have known him. Of course, he always wears a cowboy hat.

Beverly is a slender, willowy, beautiful gal, always dressed in western clothes and, like Wil, in high top boots with pants down

Wil and Beverly Howe, excellent horse trainers from Richland, Oregon.

in the boots. They make a striking pair when you see them afoot or horseback.

Wil and Beverly and I have become friends over the years. They invite me to everything they do: their seminars and clinics and schools. I enjoy their method of training.

When I first met them they had a training stable in Sisters, Oregon. At that time they made their living training horses for other people—show horses or snaffle bit horses—and selling a few of their own. They did that for several years after I knew them.

They then moved to Medford where they had a training stable with around fifty horses in each barn.

After that they went to Loomis, California, and worked with snaffle-bit horses. They were successful but they wanted to slow down. They went up to Richland, Oregon, near Baker City and close to Hells Canyon and bought a small ranch. Their pasture borders Eagle Creek.

Wil and Beverly now make their living mostly buying, training and selling horses plus holding their training clinics and classes. Normally they have more orders than they have horses.

Wil is the best man I have ever seen with a horse. He is a

horse psychologist. He gets the horse to do what he wants it to do without pain, without whipping. I have seen trainers that whipped horses so hard the horses were scared to death of them. Wil would not allow that kind of behavior on his place.

If Wil gets a two- or three-year-old horse that hasn't been spoiled, he can have that horse under saddle in just a few days. If he has to, he can have him under saddle the first day.

A horse that Wil trains does not know how to buck. He is trained not to buck and he never knows what buck is. Most of the old time trainers would turn out horses that bucked. But half of those horses simply had had a saddle thrown on them and had been bucked out to start with. That's not the way Wil and Beverly go about it.

Wil and Beverly think ground work is the single most important phase of a horse's training. They get him used to everything under the sun. When Wil first steps up on a horse, that horse has had his ground work.

Their main tool in training horses is a round pen. The pen is exactly fifty-feet in diameter, is six feet high with five rails and is too high to jump. There are no corners. There is no place for a horse to escape. In a square or rectangular corral or pasture, a horse is going to look for a way out.

Wil stands in the middle of a round pen with a long whip, which is not used as a whip, but, as Wil explains it, "as an extension of my arm." He controls the horse from the center of the ring. The horse can't get away from that guy in the middle.

Wil runs around the ring in a small circle. He says, "That horse thinks I can outrun him." As he puts it, a horse is not in the speed reading class in school. A horse is an animal that operates on instinct and for his own safety. A horse is not a fighter; he's a runner. A horse's defense, unless he is cornered, is simply to run away. And he can outrun most anything that gets after him. If a horse is cornered, he will fight back. A thousand- or fifteen-hundred-pound horse can be a dangerous adversary.

When Wil has a new horse in the round pen and the horse is running around looking for a way out and Wil is standing in the middle, he says, "Who do you think is going to win? This is a game that's called 'Wil wins.'" And that is the truth. It is a game that Wil wins.

People bring their own horses to Wil's seminars. Many are spoiled, coddled horses. I will always remember one beautiful paint

Wil Howe uses the round pen to train a horse.

gelding, four years old. He was a big horse, too fat and spoiled rotten. The lady that brought him explained that she had probably spoiled him. When Wil was through with that colt, he was a different horse.

Wil took the horse in the round pen and pulled off his halter. He said, "I want this colt to feel as free as he can feel in here. But I'm still going to control him from the center of this pen."

That colt started running around next to the fence as fast as he could, bucking and jumping and looking for a way out. When the horse finally faced him—instead of turning his rump—Wil walked over and rubbed his neck a minute. Then he walked back to the center of the ring with the horse following. He had accepted Wil as his leader.

Wil grabs hold of a horse's mind as much as anything else. The big spoiled Quarter horse paint left there like a trained dog. Wil told the woman, "Now, look, if you go back and do the same things and let him get by with murder, you'll come back to my next seminar and we'll do this over again. But you can keep him like he is. It's up to you and it's simple."

Wil has about seven or eight big railroad ties set in concrete. They stand straight up. On each one of those is a chain at the top, bolted into the railroad tie and a big bull snap on the end of the chain. The chain is about eighteen inches long.

I've seen people bring horses in and say, "Well, my horse won't tie. He'll pull back and break the rope."

Wil says, "He'll tie." Wil ties him to this immovable object and lets the horse fight. He can't hurt himself. The horse fights it for awhile and skins himself up a little. When it's all over, the horse will stand tied for as long as you need him to stand tied.

This is the way a horse ought to be. A horse you cannot tie and be satisfied with, you might as well sell to somebody who does not know the difference. I would not have a horse I could not tie. Tying is one of the first things a horse learns at Wil's place.

Wil has the simplest method for loading a balky horse. Wil loads the horse and it might take five minutes or twenty minutes. Once the horse is loaded, Wil doesn't close the door. He unloads him. He loads and unloads that horse until, when he brings that horse up to the trailer, he walks right on in and stands there until he asks him to get out. Once Wil puts him through a session, the horse loads forever unless he is let to have his own way.

I have seen Wil teach a horse to load many times. One memorable time was at a Hermiston horse sale. The sale usually gets over Sunday night around midnight or later. We were camped there in our motorhomes and were having coffee in my rig on Monday morning.

Here were two fellows who had bought two yearling colts. They were trying to load them into a two-horse trailer. They got behind them and tried to push them in. Then they tried to pull them in. They loaded hay and grain to tempt them in, then put the whip behind them to scare them in. They were trying everything.

I looked at Wil and said, "Isn't it about time we went over there?"

He said, "Yeah, I guess."

We walked over and Wil told the guys, "Look fellows this is my business. I'm a horse trainer. I'll load those colts for you and I'll teach you how to do it and I'll guarantee they'll load from here on." He said, "However, it'll cost you fifty dollars a horse."

One guy said, "Fifty dollars a horse. No way, no way. Too

much."

Wil said, "We'll be over there for another fifteen or twenty minutes if you change your mind."

We went back to my rig and in about ten minutes here came one of the fellows. He said, "Okay."

Wil said, "I'm glad to see you here because you've got those colts all skinned up now."

Wil went over and had them both loaded within twenty minutes. He had them to where he would lead them up to the trailer, throw the lead shank over their back and they would walk right in.

Since I saw Wil's horse loading method years ago, I have used it a lot and never had it fail.

Wil always used to have several stallions in his stable. As I have said, stallions are treacherous. You should never trust one. They can attack you; they can be vicious. But in Wil's barn you walk into any stall, including that of a stallion, and the horse turns around with its rump in the corner and its head facing you, and with a good attitude. Not one horse lays its ears back. It stands there. It doesn't come up and rub all over you.

Wil and Beverly give seminars around the Northwest and they are reasonably priced. A horseman, whether novice or expert, who goes to a Wil Howe seminar with an open mind and follows Wil's instructions, learns a lot about training horses. When you see Wil's methods, you wonder why you have been doing it the hard way. I am not going to try to explain what they do, but they teach you how to train a horse with nothing but good habits.

Wil has a ten-step program that he teaches. If you follow Wil's ten steps exactly as he teaches them, you can train almost any horse. Some horses are much more trainable than others, of course. Those that have been spoiled are the hardest to train.

Wil and Beverly hold three to six schools each summer at their place. They take eight students for a week and each student brings one or two horses. Wil calls it boot camp and that's what it is. They work hard for a week on how to train their horse, with Wil and Beverly right there on the ground working with them. They have a lot of fun and those who try come out knowing what they are doing.

I have an open invitation to Wil and Beverly's schools and seminars. I am the only spectator allowed at the schools and I go to a lot of them. I've attended more than twenty of Wil's seminars.

Wil and a group of students enjoy a campfire after a day at the Wil Howe School of Fine Horse Training.

As many times as I've been to a school or seminar, I enjoy each one as if it were the first. I always pick up something new.

The people who go to Wil's school take their horses with them and come out with well trained horses and know how to keep them that way. It's as important to know how to keep them trained as it is to know how to train them.

Wil and Beverly advertise their activities in the *Cascade Horseman* and sometimes in the *Western Horseman*. The seminars are good for anyone, from a beginner to those who have been around horses all their lives.

Wil goes to seminars himself when he gets a chance. If he knows a trainer who is good and is putting on a seminar, he will go and see if there is anything that he is missing. This is the mark of a good man. There is always a better way of doing things.

Wil and Beverly also have their own brand of tack that they have designed themselves. It is excellent and good for horses of all ages. They have training reins, headstalls, hobbles and a noseband that is not a cavesson. Wil's noseband is a small loop that goes around the horse's nose just bigger than the horse's head. If a horse opens his mouth, he bumps into the noseband. The noseband is not tight. It is an excellent training device to keep a horse's mouth closed, which it should be.

When Wil and Beverly were in Medford, they bought a half-grown Brahma calf. He weighed about nine hundred pounds at that time. They started training him.

Blue Boy has grown up now and weighs about twenty-four hundred pounds and is six feet tall at the withers. Wil has him so well trained that he's just a big gentle teddy bear. Wil has trained him to ride under saddle with a bit in his mouth and a bridle. Wil can saddle him up and canter on him. He takes him to the Pendleton Roundup where he is always a favorite.

Wil has said if he had to give up every animal on his ranch, Blue Boy would be the one who had to stay. Wil goes out into the pasture and calls him and he comes ambling over. Blue Boy is a big attraction wherever he goes.

Wil Howe and Blue Boy, his Brahma.

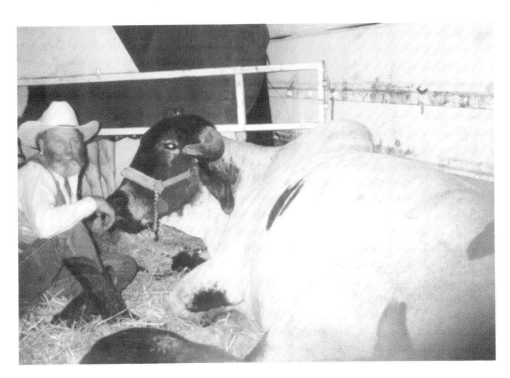

I spend quite a bit of time at Wil and Beverly's place in Richland. When they first moved in they had just the acreage and a barn. They built a log cabin, which a couple of contractors worked on for over a year. They used many unique ideas on it and wound up with one of the most beautiful log cabins that I have ever seen.

The house sits on a little knoll to the side of the barn where they can overlook all the horse pens and the barn. It overlooks Eagle Creek. The movie *Paint Your Wagon* was filmed on Eagle Creek about five miles above where Wil and Beverly's place is.

Wil and Beverly make a tremendous team. Both are excellent riders and trainers. They find a horse that has been spoiled and take him home. They start him in the round pen, tie him up and go through their ten steps of training. When they are through, he is trained. If it is a horse they can't pull out of being spoiled, they won't sell it as a trained saddle horse. They guarantee all their horses. A horse trained by Wil and Beverly would be one that any horseman would love to ride.

Wil and Beverly Howe on the porch of their log cabin in Northeast Oregon.

Epilogue

I have been a pleasure horseman all my life and I have been lucky to have had many good experiences with horses and good friends.

Those of you who are horsemen and like to ride understand immediately what I have been talking about. I have never gotten tired of horses and horse camping. I am over eighty years old and I have done it all my life. It's part of my life.

I gave up many other forms of entertainment for myself and for my family simply because I had neither the time nor the money to have all the bad habits in the world.

I did like to fish and to hunt. I like the outdoors. At one time I played golf and at one time I started to take flying lessons. But I realized that I could not do all those things. So I had to ask, what is number one with me? Number one for me was horses and that's just the way it has turned out.

As I look at my journals, my notes on camping and the fun we have had, I would love to do it all over again. It has been very rewarding.

Red Harper, Frank Riley, Whitey Ford, Art Middleton, Sid Murray, Glenn Sitz, Jim Gardner and Gale Struckmeyer have all passed away. Some of my best horses, including Rusty, Blackie, Carlos and Gentleman Jack, have all gone to greener pastures.

Guy Beck is over ninety years old and still lives in Garden Home. Bill and Carol Robertson have retired and live in Ontario, Oregon. The Rod and Rex Robertson families are still ranching in Otis Valley.

Bob and Polly Eastman have moved back to Twin Falls, Idaho, which is their home town. They bought a five-acre spot with a barn on it. He called me just the other day to say he bought another horse. He was as tickled as any young kid with a brand new wagon.

Larry and Pat Kelley moved to Helena, Montana, from Wilsonville and lived and rode horses there for six years. They are now in Salem, Oregon.

I am doing pretty well with the exception of my bad back, which put me afoot from horseback riding about fifteen years ago. Grace and I are still in Wilsonville.

I still go up to Rod and Debbie Robertson's ranch in Drewsey. I am part of the crew, although I don't ride. When we take the cattle to the mountains, I drive the pickup and pull a large stock trailer to haul cowboys and horses and be part of the scene.

I spend a lot of time at Wil and Beverly Howe's.

My summer will be gone before I know it.

Horse sense

Here are suggestions that will make you a better horseman; some might save your life or your horse's life.

Don't ever—
- Tie a horse up by the bridle reins.
- Tie your horse to a tree on public lands.
- Tie your horse to any part of a pickup or automobile.
- Tie your horse to anything that is easily damaged.
- Let your horse eat with a bit in his mouth.
- Let him drink too much water when he is hot and sweating.
- Put a hot horse away without cooling him out.
- Feed more than a token of grain when he is not working.
- Hand feed him.
- Run or gallop a horse toward the barn or camp.
- Gallop your horse into a group of riders unexpectedly.
- Ride your horse closer than eight feet behind another horse when on the trail.
- Leave your barn or horse trailer without a spare rope hanging on your saddle.
- Ride with anything but riding boots. They will come off in case of a hangup.
- Use lace-up boots.
- Ride your horse with a loose flank cinch.
- Turn your horse out with a halter on.

Bibliography

Gold and Cattle Country, Herman Oliver, Binfords & Mort, 1962

Horse Camps, Oregon Information Center, Suite 177, 800 N.E. Oregon Street, Portland, OR 97232

Oregon Desert, E.R. Jackman, R.A. Long, The Caxton Printers, Caldwell, Idaho, 1964

Oregon Geographic Names, Lewis A. McArthur, Oregon Historical Society Press, 1992

Index

A

Adair, John 17, 65, 84, 88, 166, 173
Adair, Pearl 17, 84
aging horses 112
Albright, Lola 51
Alder Springs 166, 168, 174, 179
Allen, Gerald 130
Anderson Springs 171
Antelope Swale 130, 138
Ashby, Jack 4

B

badger 146
badger hole 147, 199
Bald Mountain shelter 44
Baldy 2, 11
barn sour 2, 32
bear 146, 155, 169
Bear Springs 130, 133
Beck, Bob 11
Beck, Guy 11, 17, 27, 39, 40, 43, 58, 59, 72, 74, 77, 79, 84
Beck, Lessie 11, 84
Beers, Jack 87
Beers, Mike 87
bees 76
Benjamin Lake 204
Bill 24
Billingsley Horse Sale 212
Black Canyon 143
Blackie 76, 90, 194, 203
Blackjack 84
Blue Boy 219
Bluebucket cabin 139
Bluebucket Cow Camp 130, 131, 133, 138, 150
B'nanza Horse Sales 212
Bo Jangles 91

Bonney, Garth 25, 105
Bonnie 19
bosal 103
Boyce, Lyle 80
Brahma 219
branding 162, 163, 164
breast collar 104
bridle
  bit 102
  broken 103
  curb strap 102
  reins 102
Brown's Well 206, 210
bulls, driving 180
Buttermilk Allotment 170, 180

C

caesarean 190
calving 190
Camp Sherman 48
camping out 11, 16, 21, 61
Carey, Harry, Jr. 59
Carlos 26, 29
Carlton, Dianne 2, 11, 25, 40
Carlton, Grace 18
Carlton, Pat 1, 19, 24, 25, 82
Carpenter, Derrick 142, 150, 151
Cast Creek trail 43, 84
Cast Lake 43
Cat Creek 170, 174
Cathedral Ridge 44
cattle
  branding 162, 163, 164
  counting 128, 171
  dewlap 142
  dogs 146, 153, 177
  driving 135, 176, 200
  ear mark 142
  feeding 182
  gathering 123